BASIC ✺ ESSENTIALS™
WOMEN IN THE OUTDOORS

Help Us Keep This Guide Up to Date

Every effort has been made by the author and editors to make this guide as accurate and useful as possible. However, many things can change after a guide is published—new products and information become available, regulations change, techniques evolve, etc.

We would love to hear from you concerning your experience with this guide and how you feel it could be improved and be kept up to date. While we may not be able to respond to all comments and suggestions, we'll take them to heart and we'll also make certain to share them with the author. Please send your comments and suggestions to the following address:

The Globe Pequot Press
Reader Response/Editorial Department
P.O. Box 480
Guilford, CT 06437

Or you may e-mail us at:

editorial@globe-pequot.com

Thanks for your input, and happy travels!

BASIC ESSENTIALS™ SERIES

BASIC ✳ ESSENTIALS™

WOMEN IN THE OUTDOORS

SECOND EDITION

JUDITH NIEMI

The
Globe
Pequot
Press

Guilford, Connecticut

Basic Essentials is a trademark of The Globe Pequot Press.

Cover photo © PhotoDisc
Cover design by Lana Mullen
Text and layout design by Casey Shain
Photo credits: All photographs are courtesy of Judith Niemi, except for the photos on pages 4 and 50, which are reprinted courtesy of the Minnesota Historical Society.

Basic Essentials is a trademark of The Globe Pequot Press.

Library of Congress Cataloging-in-Publication Data
Niemi, Judith.
 Basic essentials: Women in the outdoors/by Judith Niemi.—2nd ed.
  p. cm. — (Basic essentials series)
 Rev. ed. of: The basic essentials of women in the outdoors. c1990.
 Includes bibliographical references and index.
 ISBN 0-7627-0526-4
 1. Outdoor recreation for women. 2. Women naturalists. I. Niemi, Judith. Basic essentials of women in the outdoors. II. Title. III. Title: Women in the outdoors.
GV191.64.N54 1999   99-36413
796'.082—dc21   CIP

Manufactured in the United States of America
Second Edition/First Printing

Contents

Preface to the Second Edition

Ten years ago, when I wrote the first *Basic Essentials of Women in the Outdoors,* the essentials I had in mind were not skills and gear but ideas and attitudes. I'd been guiding women's trips for almost fifteen years, and I knew the main obstacle for many women who wanted to camp, canoe, or walk in the mountains was simply that they'd been told they shouldn't or been taught inappropriately.

Since then the outdoor scene has been changing remarkably: There are more adventure-travel companies, more people involved, more gear, more information. There are also more high-profile women athletes and adventurers, more programs and gear designed for women, more women's books. I'm still happily leading women's trips, and as far as I can see, a basic problem hasn't changed much for a lot of women. They are intimidated, or put off, by the public face of outdoor adventure. They long to get closer to the natural world, but haven't found their way in.

This thoroughly revised second edition takes account of all this new information, and directs women to the resources available. It is focused on sorting out basic questions: how to get started, how to think about outdoor life, how a woman can not just join in, but live her outdoor life in her own way.

So many people are already exploring our small remnants of wild country that I hesitate to encourage any more to join us— for selfish reasons, and for the sake of our overvisited wild places. But for the good of the planet and our own souls, it's important that women and men do know wild places, and have a personal relationship with the nonhuman world. Men are, of course, welcome to read along—the specific resources and information lists are directed to women, but all of us need to think about the purpose of recreation, the meaning of our outdoor life.

—Judith Niemi

Part I:
Planning for an Outdoor Life

What's Different about Women in the Outdoors?

The best gift of the Rocky Mountains is nothing less than the transformation of life. Therefore my advice is instant to all inquirers: Go, by all means, go! ... Camp out a little for practice, if possible; if not, go just the same. You will reach heaven a better person.

—Zephine Humphrey, "Five Women on the Trail,"
Outing magazine, 1909

Women belong in wild places. The time we spend in the mountains, on the waterways, or even in nearby state parks makes us happier, rowdier, bolder, more uppity. More our true selves. Too bad many women haven't had a chance to learn this.

For more than twenty years, I've been guiding women's trips, in the North Woods, the Arctic, occasionally in the Amazon, or in deserts. The women on these trips come with a lot of outdoor experience, or none at all, but they bring the essentials: adaptability and awareness, respect for the natural world and each other. They are full of fun, and together we've learned a lot about what works for women learning outdoor skills.

I've also spent a lot of time on the telephone talking with women who are very hesitant to come on a trip: "I don't want to hold others back." "I'm afraid I'm too out of shape [or: old, overweight, inexperienced, wimpy]." Sometimes I'm just answering questions, a kind of information and referral service: "I got the canoe in the divorce, but I can't lift that sucker alone. Can you show me how?" "I'm supposed to go backpacking early next month, but I'll have my period then. What about bears?"

Where Does This Book Come In?

This book is based on those joyous experiences and those questions. It's a mixed bag of tips, lists, advice, referrals, preaching, and a lot of opinion. Some of its main ingredients:

Troubleshooting. Several supposed problems come up—not because I think they're difficulties for women, but because some people think they are. I try to answer a lot of the doubts I've heard over time. There are too many unnecessary rules out there, too, for how you're supposed to do outdoor life, and I'll suggest ignoring them.

Skills and instruction. Skills aren't really the main problem for women. Isn't building a fire or using a compass pretty much gender-free? Well, yes and no. While there are a few technical differences based on size, strength, and previous training, there are *a lot* of differences in learning style. This small book covers a few detailed techniques and many general principles. It points out where and how to learn skills, especially when instruction is slanted toward women. It mentions some special aptitudes of women.

Styles and preferences. Some women think they don't like camping when it's only that they didn't care for the style of camping they were introduced to. A true example, so extreme it's almost parody: My friend Patty found that her husband just could not leave his Type A self at the office. Even canoeing, he was always checking his watch, timing their crossing of a lake, jotting down an ETA for the next portage, the number of minutes the trail would take. Fortunately, she was the more experienced canoeist, and she finally refused to let him come with her; he eventually reformed.

Gear. There are times that women's gear is, or should be, different. This book points out a few cases where this is true, and brings up some questions to ask when you're trying to get outfitted properly.

Resources and reading. The lists are not comprehensive, but there's enough to start you down many trails. The suggested readings are not only practical but also historical and literary. I've learned a lot that matters to me about wilderness from essays and travel stories—lore, perspective, and feeling part of a long tradition of adventurous outdoorswomen.

What "ladies" wear to bike: circa 1890s, the Minneapolis Women's Walking Club; and circa 1990s, on the Noatak River, Alaska.

Taking the Long View

Before getting into any details of outdoor recreation as practiced by (some) Americans at the end of the twentieth century, let's take a moment to put this whole business of "outdoor life" in perspective.

Most of the human beings who have walked this planet haven't lived in permanent houses with porcelain plumbing and mechanical transportation. *Outdoors* is such an odd word. Why should we assume that the norm is life in a box, and that spending time out under the sky is the exception? "Camping out" is often just relearning things our foremothers had to know, things women in other parts of the world do all the time.

It's only when some people get enough wealth to invent an idea like "leisure" that outdoor life becomes "recreation," and we start to seek out more elaborate ways to do it. In this country, for example, the turn of the nineteenth century was a time when various outdoor activities (often referred to as "manly pursuits") became popular and fashionable. Hunting and fishing, basic survival techniques, became sport; canoeing, a necessity for exploration, became a weekend pleasure. There was ambivalence about women having these pleasures. Among rural nonleisured classes women had plenty of outdoor life, but ladies weren't supposed to do the more strenuous sports. (Ladies did, of course, when they could get away with it.) In recent decades there has been another huge burst of interest in outdoor recreation and adventure travel. Women's programs began springing up in the 1970s, but that was hardly the beginning, just a time of outdoorswomen getting organized. Women have been traveling adventurously all along.

If you were brought up to feel nervous about roughing it or survival, try to think more broadly. Instead of imagining explorers or adventurers, think of the native people who lived in the wilderness, only they didn't call it that—they called it home. It wasn't just the young and tough and male who had an outdoor life, it was men, women, aged people, infants. They not only survived, they often lived very well. Or go back in your own family until you come to a great-grandmother who knew herbs, or did physical work you find hard to imagine. Or just go back to your own childhood when, if you were lucky, you climbed trees and talked to animals.

These days perhaps the most visible portrayal of outdoor life comes through advertising, and that, of course, is full of drama and style: Hard-bodied young men and women dangle from bright ropes over immense drops. Tough people (and tough but sleek cars) leap streams and pose against stark mesas. Mountain bikes and snowboards catch air. It almost obscures the quieter, more democratic sort of outdoor life available to the rest of us. This book is less dramatic, because it's intended for the beginner and for any woman, regardless of size, shape, or age. But it's not about "Powderpuff Camping." Once you get started, there's no telling where you'll go.

Travel Companions and Teachers

I turned down so many people who wanted to travel with me. Being alone, and a person my age, I have so many advantages.

—Helen Broomell, canoeing the Yukon River at sixty-five; from "Solo on the Yukon" in *Rivers Running Free,* 1997

Finding the right people to go camping with can be an obstacle even for experienced outdoorswomen. In fact, depending on your age and social group, you may encounter resistance and hostility. People who wouldn't dream of criticizing your taste in food, clothing, theater, or cars hear of your plan to go rafting or hiking and say, "Are you nuts? What do you know about it?" If you really don't know anything about it, finding the right people to teach and encourage you is especially important. This chapter is a quick overview of some ways to get connected.

Kid Stuff

Maybe you started learning outdoor skills as a child; if not, it's never too late. I've watched a lot of women—and men—become about ten years old again on outdoor trips. In fact, the playfulness of a child might be better the second time around. You can combine adult knowledge and power with an emerging spontaneity and sheer silliness that's hard to express in city life.

If you're the adult traveling with children, however, the balance changes. You get very grown up and have to put their needs first, in distance, scheduling, even food. Even with quite grown children, many parents find it most satisfying to take them separately, one at a time, so each child gets special attention. Experienced outdoorswomen find ways to take their kids along even in infancy, or in utero. If you are yourself a novice, this may be a good reason to travel with a group—for safety and peace of mind, and so that your child will have other kids to be with, which takes some pressure off the parent-child interactions. Your kids may teach you a lot about enjoying the outdoors.

On the other hand, if you are just learning, you probably want some time to be a free kid yourself, and that means leaving the kids at home. Every year a number of women on our trips tell me this is their swap: Their husbands go fishing with the guys, and they get women's time out. (Think what a great example you're setting for your kids.) For that matter, I offer the same advice to outdoor leaders. No matter how much we love our work, it *is* work, and when we are guiding trips we don't get to—well, be as free and silly and push ourselves and take chances. Any outdoor leader, I think, ought to spend as least as much outdoor time on her own as she does guiding. We all need time outdoors to focus not on other people but on where we are, and perhaps to do things—get lost, travel after dark—that a responsible guide or parent probably wouldn't do.

Getting Older

When their kids are grown or their careers established is when many women have the time and resources for travel. Many then ask themselves, "Am I crazy to think I can take up a new sport at forty?" (Or fifty, or sixty . . .) Absolutely not. I've watched many women step into a canoe for the first time at sixty, or seventy, and have a fine time. (Our oldest participant was ninety-two, but then she came with her daughter, sixty-five, and slept in a bed.) Some trips, and some entire programs, are designed for older people. On many women's programs it's not unusual to find that most of the group is over fifty, even traveling in the Arctic or learning whitewater.

Illness and Disabilities

While these certainly impose some limits on outdoor activity, you shouldn't rule it out. The literature of the outdoors includes stories of blind trekkers, wheelchair mountaineers, and people who took to outdoor life to recover their health. There are some programs designed for people with disabilities and the "temporarily able-bodied." Other programs whose emphasis is not on athletic prowess but nature awareness or community might be suitable; it's worth calling them for an honest discussion of your limitations and the nature of the trip.

Singing in the rain, in raft and klepper.

Finding Teachers

Family and friends can be the most fun or the most difficult companions. If you haven't camped together before, check out your camping compatibility carefully. You know, ask some questions like: "What's your idea of 'early'? How many hours a day do you want to be moving on? Why? What's your pet peeve on trips?" If you're reading this book, you probably don't already have a wide circle of camping friends, but you may know people who can help you get started. Since they may or may not be skilled teachers, talk over what you need in an introductory trip. You might consider asking someone to teach you (they may be flattered) and picking up the expenses for a short trip where that's the main purpose.

Informal volunteer organizations. Call local colleges, check bulletin boards of outdoor stores, and look up some of the resource organizations in the appendix. These groups organize low-cost trips, sometimes provide equipment, and may be a good way to meet outdoor people. They may also provide some teaching, but don't assume this. Beginners, understandably, expect or hope to learn skills. The old-timers, meanwhile, may have become a somewhat closed group, perhaps without that intention; it may take some time to break into their ranks, so don't take it personally. It could just be they are out to enjoy themselves with other experienced people and hadn't counted on teaching. Find out what the leaders intend, and whether the trips are rated in terms of difficulty or speed of travel.

Adventure-travel companies or outdoor programs can be the most expensive way to travel, but they often offer not only expertise but professional instruction as well. Their style and goals should be well defined, so read carefully everything in their brochures (and between the lines), and ask questions. Will they teach you outdoor skills or do they emphasize fine food and entertainment? Which do you want? Do they focus on learning about nature? on building your character through challenge? on fun? Call them and ask so you don't discover that while you wanted to learn route finding, the guides won't even let you look at the maps, or that you're the only middle-aged woman with a group of college boys. (Friends of mine have had both these experiences.) What kind of people typically come on their trips? Be honest about your own fitness, experience, and fears. Do you get concrete answers to your questions about the difficulty of the trip, or just assurance that you'll do fine? Don't be shy about asking for references or information on their guides. How long have they been in business? How long have they been doing the kind of trip you are interested in?

Women's programs and networks. Twenty-some years ago, almost the only all-women's trips were offered by small companies or groups organized for that purpose. Several organizations in the 1970s, when their women instructors proposed some women-only trips, said, "What on earth for? Do it on your own time." But outdoor recreation has been an amazing growth business, and these days you can find women-only trips within almost any kind of outdoor program. If a company does not specialize in women's trips, a good question to ask them is how their women's trips are different from their others. (To get a good answer on this, you may have to ask to talk to one of the guides; the people in the office may not know.)

Women's programs differ greatly. (Some of the ways I think we're alike are in the next chapter.) Some people assume all women's programs spend endless time on consensus and "process" (not true). Or that "women's trip" is code for "lesbian trip"; if the brochure doesn't say "lesbians only," you can assume that all women are welcome. (I've found that trips can vary from mostly lesbians to mostly heterosexual women to any proportion—and no one really cares.) Women's trips could be about goddesses or about animal tracks, about hardcore skills or women's history. It's just a matter of finding what's compatible with your wishes.

Women in the Outdoors   **9**

Separate and Equal?—Women's Trips versus Mixed Groups

You may or may not have strong preferences about this. If you have a choice and are uncertain, here are a few reasons for choosing one or the other.

Sarah Harrison, who has spent decades leading adult and youth trips, sees good reasons for both co-ed and women's trips. "Especially for girls about fourteen, or fifteen, it can be so important for them to do it all themselves, to know they are capable and don't need the young men. With somewhat older kids, a mixed trip can be a first opportunity to work together; they come out with a great deal of regard for each other. We've all got to live in this world together."

Of the adult trips she's led, she says that women's trips have "a special kind of community and intimacy." But sometimes, as on a "life/career renewal course," it's more important to talk with a variety of people who are dealing with similar questions.

Learning styles are likely to be different on all-women's trips. Women ask more questions than men, are more likely to want to understand an activity before leaping in, and both expect and offer a lot of support. There's also likely to be a difference in how the group operates. I asked Janet Ross, who offers many co-ed trips and a few women's trips at Four Corners Outdoor School, how she would advise a woman to choose between two trips that were otherwise exactly the same. "Well," she said, "if a woman wants things to operate according to plan, to know just what's scheduled for each day, she'll probably be happiest on a trip with men and women. If she wants a trip that's a bit more flexible, accommodates weather and people's individual wishes, she should come on a women's trip."

Solo Travel

This may seem an odd note in a book of basics, when some books warn even experienced campers against *any* solo wilderness travel. And I'm not suggesting you terrify yourself and risk your life. (Be sure to check out chapter 4, Being Afraid.) Still, at whatever level you are comfortable outdoors, the time you spend alone will probably be your most intense, and you'll learn the most. You aren't out to prove anything, just to enjoy the natural world undistracted. I don't know any woman who's done solo travel who wouldn't say, "Go!"

Ladies' Day?

Some of you want to stop and lounge around for a day, while others would rather explore a side route; some want to get up with the dawn and be traveling in the cool while others like a leisurely breakfast. Dividing up for a while (I don't, of course, mean that the men get to catch fish and the women get to cook them) works wonders to reduce any stresses being built up in a group—it's a nice change of pace. It can be very difficult to get people to agree to it, though. Obviously, you need to be sure it's safe to divide up, and to have flexible and foolproof plans for reconnecting. Still, I suspect the real reason groups don't divide is not the practical problems, but an unspoken rule of togetherness. And of all the ways of dividing, by gender is probably the touchiest one.

Whether you're just out with friends or have signed up for a trip whose leaders are open to suggestions, if you think some separate activities (by gender, age, whatever) would make the trip more fun, start *early*, before the habit of compulsory togetherness grows too strong to break. You don't always need to divide up the same way. And don't feel guilty; you aren't rejecting the other people, just choosing more freedom and, often, more peace and quiet.

Resources

FOR FURTHER READING

Consult Jan Brown's *Women Outdoors Bibliography* (see the appendix) for categories including family adventures, older women, and women with disabilities. Here are a few of the books available:

Gabbard, Andrea. *No Mountain Too High: A Triumph over Breast Cancer*. Seattle: Seal Press, 1998. Story of the climb of Aconcagua by seventeen survivors of cancer.

Gould, Jean, ed. *Season of Adventure: Traveling Tales and Outdoor Journeys of Women Over 50*. Seattle: Seal Press, 1996.

Lee, Elaine, ed. *Go Girl! The Black Woman's Book of Travel and Adventure*. Portland, Oreg.: Eighth Mountain Press, 1997.

Rogers, Susan Fox, ed. *Another Wilderness: New Outdoor Writing by Women*. Seattle: Seal Press, 1997.

———. *Solo: On Her Own Adventure*. Seattle: Seal Press, 1996.

Warren, Karen, ed. *Women's Voices in Experiential Education*. Kendall/Hunt, 1996. Twenty-five essays by women working with survivors of abuse, other special programs.

dition Inspiration. VCR; 60 minutes. $25, from Breast Cancer Fund, Second Street, Second Floor, San Francisco, CA 94105; (415) 545-2979. The story of the Aconcagua climb (see Gabbard, above).

Our Feet on the Ground: Changing through Cancer. VCR; 30 minutes. $32.95 (including postage and handling), from On the Ground, P.O. Box 7244, St. Paul, MN 55107; (800) 343-5540. Produced by Women in the Wilderness, the Women's Cancer Resource Center, Fourth Canyon Production, and Image Electric. Six cancer survivors talk about nature and healing while canoeing, dogsledding, and climbing.

PROGRAMS FOR WOMEN

Women Outdoors (see the appendix) publishes a directory of women's programs nationwide. It's a good starting point though it's not always up to date. Once you're in contact with one program, if they don't offer the trips or classes you want, ask for recommendations. You'll find most of us are very willing to pass on information and do some networking for you.

The Resources sections in chapters 9 and 10 include books that can direct you to specific programs in canoeing, hiking, and so on. You can also consult books oriented to (mostly international) adventure travel:

Davies, Miranda, and Natania Jansz, eds. *Women Travel: Adventures, Advice and Experience.* London: Rough Guides, 1994.

Zepatos, Thalia. *Adventures in Good Company: The Complete Guide to Women's Tours and Outdoor Trips.* Portland Oreg.: Eighth Mountain Press, 1994.

———. *A Journey of One's Own: Uncommon Advice for the Independent Woman Traveler.* Portland, Oreg.: Eighth Mountain Press, 1992.

Two annual directories of resources, including some outdoor programs, are:

Places of Interest to Women. Ferrari Publications, P.O. Box 37887, Phoenix, AZ 85069; (602) 863-2408.

Women's Traveller. P.O. Box 422458, San Francisco, CA 94142-2458.

SPECIAL-FOCUS PROGRAMS
FOR WOMEN AND MEN

Elderhostel. 75 Federal Street, Boston, MA 02110; (617) 426-8056.

Wilderness Inquiry. 1313 Fifth Street SE, Box 84, Minneapolis, MN 55414-1546; (800) 728-0719 (voice or TTY). www.wildernessinquiry.org. Adventurous trips throughout the U.S., always including people with disabilities.

Women's Ways of Having Fun

The long miles which separated me from the world did not make me feel far away—just far enough to be nice—and many times I found myself wishing I need never have to go back again.

—Mina Benson Hubbard,
A Woman's Way through Unknown Labrador, 1908

Realistic Expectations

"There we were, in Paradise, hating each other," said an experienced outdoorswoman, just back from her dream trip in the Northwest Territories. Six skilled outdoor leaders had spent six weeks seeing wonderful places, having new experiences and inner growth, but the conflicts and tensions among them were a bitter disappointment.

One of the open secrets of outdoor life is how often people have a perfectly miserable time with each other. This is true on every level, from fierce expedition rivalries to disappointing summer vacations. It's not surprising. You've planned a dream vacation, and find out that others' dreams aren't identical. Just when you want to slow down and appreciate things, someone insists on pushing on. When you want to go for it, someone is a wet blanket. Throw in egos, fears, exhaustion, and even one day of rain, and it gets hard to repair the bad feelings. We don't talk about this a lot, because usually the trips are so great in other ways. Anyway, who wants to come home and tell the neighbors that the Big Trip was a bummer?

No matter whom you go camping with—friends, family, clubs, or organizations—your best insurance against disappointment is to find out in advance if you have compatible ideas on what a trip should be like, and how flexible you all are about your wants. Also crucial is finding styles of leadership and group interaction that work for you.

Tips from Women's Trips

"Jeez, you women seem to have so much fun," men have told me. "Can't I sneak along?" They aren't being flirtatious, just genuinely wistful. The outdoor programs run by women, for women, that have sprung up in the last fifteen years have a lot of similarities in philosophy and style. This isn't because we all sat down at a conference to decide the correct way, though a lot of us do stay in touch with each other. It just evolved, naturally, from following our own ideas and seeing what works. Maybe because of this pragmatic approach, one of the things that's really common on women's trips is having a terrific time.

All-women's trips aren't automatically better than other arrangements, but they do give women a chance to find their own ways to do things. Here, wildly overgeneralized and oversimplified, are a few of the values and techniques common in women's programs; take what you can use for your own trip planning.

Inclusiveness. Women's programs often try to welcome a real variety of women—in experience, background, lifestyle, age, income, class, and race (not all of these balances are easy to achieve). The important part is to have each person feel welcome as she is, not just as a potential outdoor type. If we value the individual more than the group, enjoy the diversity, and aren't too hung up about rules, it helps. "We don't have a generation gap," said one young woman on a trip where ages ranged from twenty-five to seventy. "We just have a whole lot of information we didn't have before."

Noncompetitiveness. We can get about as much stress and competition as we want in our everyday lives. On women's trips there's rarely much emphasis on making miles or proving toughness. Difficult physical tasks don't get more status. "This is the first time I've been on a trip where the canoe carriers weren't the elite," said one woman, with relief. Little contests that come up (getting the tents up fastest in the rain, impromptu touch football with a sponge) come from spontaneous high spirits, not a plan.

We promote a noncompetitive attitude toward nature, especially when doing strenuous things. Women mountaineers don't talk of "conquering" a mountain (a pretty silly term). When we run rapids (rather than "shoot" them), I think of the river as the third partner, the strongest (and bossiest) of all of us. We aren't so much challenging nature as feeling more deeply at home.

Supportive atmosphere. My brother-in-law returned once from a

Figuring out where we are, together.

camping trip saying that the women had had more fun. Why? "They didn't seem to have expectations for themselves, so they could encourage each other and feel really satisfied when they learned to do something. Some of the guys were into proving they knew things, even if it was all new to them, so they couldn't accept any praise."

One of my friends is a hot-dog competitive kayaker; her first all-women's trip was a revelation. "It was great! I was used to running a rapids and having no one say anything. Unless you messed up—then you got razzed. But the women were always cheering each other on, 'Good run!' And when I capsized, they were still cheering, 'Great swim!'" We can get rather carried away with this. On a log-cabin building course I noticed that all work had stopped. A small woman was using a heavy maul to slam down old scaffolding, and five others had gone to be a cheering section. "Go, Deb!"

Individual choice. Most women have a healthy streak of anarchy. We're very sensitive to others in a group, but we don't take well to regimentation. In an interesting documentary film of women on a highly structured trip, the group was sent on an unguided hike for which they felt unprepared. "I feel like I'm being tested," said one

Women in the Outdoors

woman. "And I don't like it." Deciding to come on a trip or not shouldn't be the last choice you get to make. ("You're in the army now.") When challenging activities are offered, it means more if you participate out of free choice. Most women leaders try to provide a lot of encouragement, and no pressure.

Participatory leadership. A group needs leadership. It doesn't need A Leader, one guy who runs the show. Most of the daily decisions campers make don't require much expertise—how far to go tomorrow, how to put up the tarp (if it's less than perfect, people still probably learned more by deciding). An experienced leader's job is to see that everyone has the crucial information, to facilitate a decision getting made, and (here's an important part!) to see that the plans everyone helped make get carried out. In a real emergency one person takes charge, usually the designated leader or most experienced person. At other times the more people who are really thinking and deciding, the more leadership there is around. Decision making is generally shared and very flexible—anything from the leader saying, "Here's what we'll do, and why," to a full discussion of choices.

Creative leadership. Leadership is a task and function, not a matter of authority. Women guides working together may say, "You be the dad today, I'll do the mom stuff, and tomorrow we'll switch." Everyone knows what that means (who has the maps, who checks in on feelings), and the "nonleaders" see the jobs as separate from personalities.

In a "leaderless" group of friends and peers, women's reluctance to step into leadership can be a problem. One woman described it as "like sitting in a circle around the campfire—but there's no fire." Women have found ways to see that leadership gets shared around. One or two may be "on duty for the day,"—probably not in fixed

Take Me to Your Leader

Most women are comfortable with leadership as a shared responsibility, but in some outdoor circles, questioning authority can be a touchy topic. I got into a strange argument once with a noted outdoor safety instructor who insisted that a group must always have One Leader. Only minutes earlier he had been telling about the tragic death of a guide by hypothermia—no one had noticed he was becoming disoriented and acting peculiar. If the other people had been accustomed to exercising judgment and responsibility, I thought, the leader probably would not have died; certainly the "leaderless" survivors would have been much safer.

Consensus

Here's a word much misunderstood. Asking people for their opinions, giving them a chance to express wishes, does not require "consensus." True consensus means that nothing goes forward until all in the group are in agreement. It's best saved for situations where a group has common values and goals, is accustomed to working together, and is dealing with an issue of real significance—say, a group of Quakers deciding whether a boycott is justified. It is not appropriate for deciding on a lunch spot or a campsite when perhaps only the guide has the information. "False consensus" is just blackmailing people into expressing unfelt agreement. People do not expect to get all their wishes; they primarily want to be *listened to*, taken into account.

In Paradise, Hating Each Other

I suggest that the problem I noted at the beginning of this chapter was not at all incompatibility—these were women who knew and liked each other. But they were all accustomed to being the recognized leaders in a formal program; here where they were all peers, equals in experience, they failed to create an alternate form of leadership and group style to cope with the natural tensions. And once tensions build up, it's too late to feel creative.

rotation, but as nominated by others or themselves, as appropriate. One group used a lace-edged bandanna as a daily rotating award to recognize individual contributions ("superb corn bread," "good humor in spite of PMS"). On one trip everybody was made a boss of some kind. There were expected roles, like map reader, and timekeeper, but also people in charge of other important matters: a trip naturalist, a sun worshiper, a reader.

Playfulness. I'm certainly not going to tell you how to be playful. This is just a reminder that the outdoors is a perfect place to let loose the impulses that got stifled about the time people started telling us to act our age. I remember a night that the oldest women in our group got into singing old show tunes—"Honey, you've never heard of Dianna Durbin?" They were tap dancing on the sand, and the teenagers partying nearby had to ask us to pipe down. On another trip I saw a staid librarian leap down the beach, a tarp flying for a shawl, in a creditable imitation of Isadora Duncan. Silliness and seriousness go hand in hand. The most playful groups are likely to have intense and intimate conversations. That's the other side of this freedom, an openness to your most serious and perceptive self.

Tiptoeing through a tributary.

Which Life Is "Real Life"?

What results from all the ways women choose to do our outdoor lives? We find ways to become more ourselves. Camping is not a collection of skills to be mastered, but an open-ended kind of growing. Returning to the "real world" can be painful; especially on long or intense trips, it's a good idea to talk about what going back will be like, and to think about how to keep alive the lessons of the outdoors. What kind of lessons? One of the obvious ones is self-confidence. "If I did that, I can do anything."

Maybe it's creating a culture more to our liking than the one we live in. The head of a women's studies program once commented, "What we do in the classroom is the theory; what women invent together outdoors is the practice—you get to live it out." For some women the lesson is feeling like part of nature again. A woman from Brooklyn built her first fire by a northern lake and said, "I feel like I'm remembering all this."

As I was writing this, I happened into a phone conversation with a stranger in California, who described herself as a 5-foot, hundred-pound hiker. "When I'm in the mountains," she said, "is the only time I'm in a place that's *big* enough for me."

Being Afraid: Not a Bad Thing If It Doesn't Hold You Back

4

"In spite of the opposition of every friend who was on hand to register a complaint (and those at a distance objected by mail) I proceeded with preparations for riding awheel [bicycling] from Chicago to San Francisco. . . . I started amidst a chorus of prophecies of broken limbs, starvation, death from thirst, abduction by cowboys. . . ."

—Margaret Lelong, *Outing* magazine, 1898

What's Really Dangerous?

A typical scene at the beginning of a trip: We're standing on the shore of a wilderness lake, gear and expectations piled around. The guide (that's me) has just now stopped fretting about what letter I forgot to mail and anything else from city life. I'm relaxed, happy, and home. But several beginning canoeists are looking across the wide lake, watching the wind rise, biting their lips nervously. "Well," I say, "now the dangerous part of your trip is over! Driving here. From here on, we're in a pretty secure place."

Our chances of being seriously hurt on a camping trip are usually far less than in everyday life: commuting to work, for example, or climbing ladders. Yet people often assume that camping is vaguely dangerous, especially for women. We'll be criticized by others for "taking foolish risks," if these risks (unspecified) are in the wilderness.

This is sad and very ironic. Traveling in wild country you are taking calculated risks, often small ones, about matters largely under your own control. You can decide whether to climb a particular cliff; whether to ski a hill or walk down sidestepping. You can judge what's within your skill and experience. The forces of nature are powerful, dangerous sometimes, but they aren't out to get us. In our city lives, on the other hand, we are surrounded by dangers beyond our control or prediction. After a peaceful time in the wilderness, I'm really jumpy on the freeway, with cars hurtling toward me at terrifying speed, driven, for all I can tell, by maniacs. In grizzly country I carry a can of pepper spray, but I don't feel paranoid—just watchfulness. Walking alone through an empty parking ramp is far more alarming, because here there *are* people out to get me, or any woman. Still, until a headline reminds us, we often ignore the random, everyday danger of "civilized" life. How could we bear to really think about it?

Despite horrible incidents of rape and murder on trails and in national parks (most commonly in areas close to civilization), being beyond the reach of 911 may offer more safety than danger. The biggest danger generally is our own ignorance, and that is correctable. We need to learn the environment, to learn not only skills but also habits of awareness and taking responsibility. And we need to take the mystery and romance out of words like *risk* and *danger*.

Running the rapids.

BASIC ESSENTIALS

To Be Fearless, Know What You Need to Know

My friend Jesse, a botanist and paleo-ecologist, has traveled widely in the Arctic for work and pleasure. But she grew up in New York City, clueless about wild places; when she started doing field research, she says, she felt confused about danger. "Half the men I worked with told me, 'Hey, relax, nothing to worry about.' The other half liked to make everything sound dangerous, to scare me: 'Ohohoho, you're going *there*?' Now, I knew there were things to worry about, but I also knew it wasn't nearly as bad as the macho types wanted me to think." She started really enjoying the outdoors when she met people willing to talk honestly about dangers, without minimizing them and without hype.

A Recipe for Handling Fear

These suggestions are oversimplified, but practical.

Respect your own fears. Fear, after all, has great survival value. It makes us alert, sharpens our senses, gets our adrenaline going. It's just that as a novice, it's not easy to sort out reasonable fears from unnecessary ones. Notice fear, don't try to talk yourself out of it.

Don't try to cover them up. Fears are sneaky, and if you try to ignore them, they are going to show up in worse ways. You'll be so preoccupied that you get clumsy and make bad decisions. You may end up paralyzed by the (unsurveyed) size of your fears. If you try to deny that you're afraid, you could take stupid chances. At the very least, carrying around unnecessary fear is a waste of energy and spoils your fun. Fortunately, many women find it easier to admit fears than men, who generally have years of training in toughing it out. Try saying, "Hey, I am really nervous—can we talk this through?" A good outdoor teacher or friend won't laugh at you but will give you time, help you figure out what's dangerous and what's merely unfamiliar to you.

Distinguish between danger of bodily harm and fear of simply looking bad. These days we use the term *risk* for everything from racing into a burning building to simply telling an uncomfortable truth. Is injury the fear, or embarrassment?

Don't get pressured into uncomfortable situations. Better a slightly bruised ego than a broken bone, say I. Peer pressure should not overrule your own sense of what's right for you.

Be realistic about consequences. What happens if I mess up? Think of worst-case and most-likely results. A woman learning whitewater

Being intimate with rock.

canoeing woke one morning miserable with nerves, having capsized twice the day before. A little later she was smiling, all set to get back on the river. She said, "I finally remembered to ask myself the same question I ask in all the rest of my life, 'So what's the worst that could happen?' Well, considering all our safety precautions, the worst seems to be I could get real wet, and I might feel like a klutz. Big deal."

Evaluate what risks are worth taking, and why. It's a very subjective thing: Some people thrive on adrenaline, need the stimulus of risk. Many of us are pretty much averse to risk, unless something important to us is involved. There are ethical questions involved in risk taking. "Why am I doing this? Are the rewards worth it? Who else is my action affecting?"

Find practical solutions. As you gain experience you don't become fearless, you simply transfer your confidence from guides or other experienced outdoorspeople to your own judgment. You learn to foresee problems and avoid them. When I'm guiding a trip, I worry about everything in advance, in the city; then I do whatever I can to prevent any of my fears from coming true.

Many of the best accident-prevention techniques seem to come very naturally to women. Take your time. Pay attention to your body and mind; know when you're too tired for good judgment. Let things follow their own natural time. Don't get so caught up with goals that you don't notice the realities of the moment. Don't be afraid to change your plans, to "wimp out" when your common sense tells you to. Trust your hunches. The same intuition that sometimes tells you not to turn down a dark street can protect you in the wilderness.

Owning Your Fear

At the "risk" of alarming some readers, here are several examples of what I think are women's ways of being open about fear, acting responsibly about danger, and being in an extreme situation. They're from Arlene Blum's book *Annapurna* (San Francisco: Sierra Club, 1999). Climbing in the Himalayas, at the highest altitudes, is objectively very dangerous—one climber in ten doesn't come back. The year 1978, when the American women's expedition went to Annapurna, was an exceptionally bad one for avalanches. When some of the women were terrified of crossing an avalanche path, leader Blum encouraged them to take some time off, although they worried about not doing their part; in a couple of days they returned, still scared but freely choosing to be there. Most important, their fear had not become contagious.

Individual climbers often reevaluated their wish to reach the top against the high danger, and they didn't all come to the same conclusions. Irene Miller did reach the peak, but she had almost resigned, not out of fear for herself, but because her daughter, only thirteen, still needed her. Two other women who were in position to try for the summit chose not to. They valued other things more. (One had a tiny hole in her glove and was likely to lose a finger; her career was surgery. The other was newly in love.) Two others made a second, very risky summit attempt, and died. It was a tragedy for their companions, who had opposed the attempt but felt they should respect the decision of the climbers to whom the high risk seemed worth taking.

In all the tension and worry of the expedition, individual choices were consistently respected. It seems to me a sane thing not to value risk taking for itself, but to constantly examine, as the Annapurna women did, its meaning to an individual life.

Okay, so what about that rapist or mugger on the dark street, or the dark trail? Is it ever really safe for a woman to travel outdoors alone? I suppose not, but it's still safer than in the city, where human predators and potential victims are more numerous. The farther you go from civilization, the more likely it is that you've left behind a lot of dangerous people. If you travel alone—and many women do—use the same precautions you'd use anywhere else. Scout out the territory. In a public campground size up the neighbors, and let the reliable ones know you're there. If you're uncomfortable, move on. In a wild area you may prefer to simply avoid other people, camping inconspicuously.

There's Real Value in Meeting Your Own Fears

I'm not talking about ego here or feeling like heroes, just about clarity. I think one reason we think about "wilderness" and "danger" in the same breath is that the outdoors provides us with such clear and straightforward ways for us to meet our fears, and overcome them.

I remember a woman who learned canoeing in her seventies. "The day I decided to come on this trip," she said, "was the day I saw my brother lying in his casket, not having done half the things in life he always wanted to." It took some nerve for her to paddle the stern or to ride with a guide through small rapids. And right after that external experience, she took an emotional risk: She confided to new camping friends that she'd been molested by her grandfather as a child. She had told no one in sixty years.

The impact can be lasting. One day, on a long whitewater trip, when five of us were cheering and whooping it up at the bottom of tricky rapids, the sixth woman started to cry. "I feel terrible. You're all having such fun and I am scared shitless." It took courage for her to say that. Once she had, and we'd talked about it, her fears began to diminish. In a few days she was so enthusiastic about rapids that the rest of us were busy holding her back. Many months later she told me how she had come home and made major changes in her life and relationships. "I figured all that fear I had wasn't just about the water," she said. "And once I got over my excessive fear of rapids, a lot of other fears seemed to disappear with it."

Part II:

Living Outside

Better Homes and Campsites

You will always find the handiest things in life are bow knots and large safety pins.

—Constance Helmericks, *Down the Wild River North,* 1968
(a mother's advice to her teenage daughters,
during their canoe trip down the Peace,
Slave, and Mackenzie Rivers)

"Camping" can mean anything from being jammed into a tiny wind-buffeted tent at an altitude where every breath is difficult to relaxing in a palatial family tent with folding cots. My own preferences vary: sometimes only a sleeping bag under desert stars, sometimes car camping with a two-story foam pad and a bookcase in the backseat. Camping is essentially just creating some kind of temporary home, getting away from your usual one. You don't need to travel far; remote places offer special pleasures, but there's no special merit in distance. In those remote places I've met Inuit people living in a tent just a mile from their home in town—for peace and quiet, a change of pace. A friend in St. Paul sometimes pitches a tent in a state park in the spring and commutes to work. Humans do hanker for remnants of nomadic life, a new point of view.

Whether you have to fit everything into a sea kayak or have a llama or horse helping you carry, the general principles are the same: Bring along enough stuff for reasonable comfort, but not so much that it complicates life and travel. And anything you bring ought to have two or more uses.

It's Just Housekeeping

It's a well-kept secret: "Camping skill" is about 90 percent housekeeping. Most women handle these little routines like old pros, and don't even think of them as "skills." Picking up after yourself; knowing where to find the bug dope; seeing work to be done; being able to boil the tea water while you put away the day's clothing while you talk with someone. You're halfway to being a good camper if you have the habit of attention to detail. If, on the other hand, you're organizationally impaired, at least camping is easier—there's a lot less to keep track of.

A place for everything. Be compulsive. Exactly where things go doesn't matter much, as long as your flashlight is always in the same pocket, the first-aid kit in the same stuff sack, so you can find things as automatically as in your own cupboards. Carry a small day pack or a fanny pack with all the things you need to have handy during the day (raincoat, sunscreen, compass) and perhaps a few emergency items (a whistle, matches, space blanket); then you don't need to keep rummaging through all your gear for the Chapstick. (Some backpacks are now made with detachable day packs and fanny packs.) Keep it packed all the time and you'll be ready to go off on day trips on a moment's notice. Organize the campsite, too. At home I have a bad habit of littering, dropping things just anywhere, but camping I sometimes become a bush-league Martha Stewart. Expect some order and elegance, and be bossy if necessary (it will be): "No personal gear in the kitchen! That's the *dining room,* keep it clear. No laundry blocking the view!"

Learn to Make Yourself at Home Anywhere

The search for the Perfect Campsite can be frustrating. In many well-traveled areas you'll be required to stay at designated sites, so your main job isn't picking the best place, but stopping before you find NO VACANCY signs everywhere. Here's another good reason to be flexible. Don't pass up a beautiful place to camp just because your plan called for some other dot on the map, or making more miles.

A merely *very good* campsite, on the other hand, is easy to achieve if you remember that your point is to enjoy the surroundings, not found a village. As the Realtors say, it's all location, and if you're where you want to be or where you need to stop, a practical definition of a good site is 1) any safe, flat spot to sleep; 2) any old port in a storm. Flat beds, shelter, morning exposure, good drainage? All luxuries. As

The Overbuilt Camp

Camping handbooks of previous generations are full of "pioneering" activities: lashing tables, digging trenches around tents, and building elaborate balsam-bough beds. Some people still practice them. All unnecessary, and now generally recognized as inappropriate, often harmful. I suspect the real reason for all this nesting activity was insecurity—changing the face of nature to be able to lay some kind of claim to a place. These days we've largely replaced that sort of beaver work with obsessing about our tents, tarps, and correct technique. Here's a better way to fulfill this nesting impulse and make a connection with a place: *Do nothing.* If you leaned against a tree dreaming or fell asleep in the sun, a place will stay in your mind a long time.

you travel farther from the beaten path, where there are no established sites, use imagination. My friend Connie once announced cheerfully, "Oh, good! We can camp right here in the aspen glade!" when any fool could see it was a mud flat. Once we improvised a late camp in a sphagnum bog; it didn't *look* like a campsite, so some people glumly called it "a swamp," but Kathy called it "Merlin's Enchanted Forest" and loved it.

Setting Up Camp—Getting Priorities Right

To many people it seems only logical and correct to get all the camp chores done first, then relax. The old work ethic. But as always, the "work" can be counted on to fill all available time. Ignore that rule when you can—decide what you want to do first. Many people have a strong urge to get their own beds ready first of all—and why not? I've found there's no point trying to get their attention on group tasks like cooking until their tents are up and belongings stashed away. On the other hand, when some experienced campers and free spirits arrive at a campsite, they want first to wander around and explore. We might be willing to do *minor* useful tasks along the way, like picking up a few sticks of firewood, but the real point is time alone. This doesn't become a point of conflict if you clarify: "I'll be happy to fix dinner in half an hour; right now, I hear the call of the wild." And then, while the sun shines, do what's most important to you—swimming, writing in your journal, napping. Women need to stop doing so much housekeeping and taking care of other people; the point of camping isn't efficiency, it's getting out of everyday life.

At other times, however—say, when rain clouds are coming up—things need to happen fast. That's a time for a benevolent dictator to arise and clarify what's important. I've watched an entire group of

Any old port in a storm.

experienced campers get soaked, scrambling madly to put up their
tents in a downpour, when waiting fifteen or twenty minutes would
have let the squall blow through, and they and their tents would have
stayed dry. They'd have done better to get a tarp up over all the gear,
then get a stove lit and start cooking—at least soup—before everyone
was too tired to bother. Sometimes, someone needs to play mom and
order chilled and tired people into dry clothes right away. This seems
obvious but is easy to forget. I've hunched under dripping trees,
shivering and grumbling at a balky stove until someone reminded me I
was being clumsy because I'd forgotten to change clothes. Of course—
one of the early warning signs of hypothermia is stupidity.

Dividing Up Camp Tasks

In Girl Scouts we divided up camp jobs fairly by elaborate "caper
charts," but I've never seen the slightest point in formally assigning
tasks to adults. Sometimes there's a hurry and people should do what
they are best at; sometimes people want to try new things. Some
people never cook, but will wash dishes every meal. (The only woman
who ever objected, and strongly, to this casual approach was an ex-
marine, and when she came back on another trip years later, she'd
loosened up.) Women are so responsible that getting things done is
generally not a problem; more often everyone works more than

necessary. In an informal way, pay attention to how things get done, if only to be sure that people get time away without feeling guilty. "It doesn't take all six of us to cook. We need two volunteers to go watch the sunset."

Fire

To many people the campfire is the heart of camping. Some treasure sitting around the campfire singing (to the distress of others, who call for a halt to "Kumbayah"). Others gaze silently at the falling coals, evoking ancient memories of the dawn of our species. Nice as all this is, ask yourself often, "Do I need (or even want) a fire?" It's also good to be friendly with the dark, watch the stars, listen to the night sounds. And of course there are many times and places where fires are inappropriate: above tree line, anywhere fuel is scarce, anytime there's high fire danger. Cooking is often easier on a stove anyway. Buy yourself a good camp stove and learn how to use it and repair it. Anything from a Coleman Big Green Box to the tiniest Whisperlite will do—depending on your style of camping. Get advice from a knowledgeable store clerk or friend.

When fires are appropriate, build them no bigger than necessary. Afraid you'll lose face because you can't make a "one-match fire"? All fires start with one match (and good tinder, and good kindling, and patience). It's just that sometimes a lot of other matches are wasted on premature starts. Bring plenty of matches, squirreled away in several separate waterproof containers (pill bottles work fine). Fire building is a high-status skill and a popular camp chore. If you camp with others who are much better than you at fire building, con them into being your teachers. If you are a good fire builder, don't monopolize the job;

Keeping the Flame Alive

I don't think this metaphor works for men, but women understand the needs of fires when I say, "Give the fire patient attention; nurture it as you would a relationship."

◆ Start easy and build gradually. Coddle it along from tiny spark of interest, to a nice little flame, to a fire big enough to warm you. This is a process, not a one-shot task. Don't pile everything on in the first few minutes.

◆ The logs need to be close enough to share body heat. (You might also need to insulate your fire from snowy or wet ground.) But they also need space to breathe. Don't let them smother each other.

◆ Keep introducing new interests, new larger wood. Without growth, the fire will die out.

get your fun from teaching others. And if you get good at one-match fires, try using a flint and steel instead (modern versions are available at camp stores), just because it's fun.

Forbidden Skills

There are several useful camping skills that many women shy away from, ones they haven't been encouraged to learn. If any of these jobs are mysteries to you, start learning them, one at a time, from books or other people. They can be important to camp comfort, aren't particularly hard, and are mostly fun.

Splitting wood. Not chopping down trees—just splitting logs so you can start fires in any rain. For safety, get a good instructor to coach you. Start with easy wood (soft wood, short pieces). I think of it as a Zen exercise in concentration, but other women say cheerfully that they think about an ex and find splitting wood *really* therapeutic.

Sharpening your knife or ax. Just get a whetstone and oil (and a file if you are using an ax) and start practicing. Dull tools make you feel inept.

Starting the camp stove and fiddling with it to keep it going. Ninety-five percent of what gets a stove working right is pumping and more pumping. The rest is oiling gaskets and carrying a few simple parts.

Knots. When you aren't sure of your knot, don't keep adding more on top until the whole thing looks like macramé. The goal is *one* good knot that you'll guarantee (test it) and that comes easily undone when you want it to.

A Good Night's Sleep

Not sleeping well is one of the main reasons people give for not liking camping. Do whatever you have to do for good sleep. These things help:

◆ A waterproof ground cloth. If you are using a tent, use an extra plastic sheet inside the tent, extending up the tent wall a few inches.

◆ A sleeping pad. Self-inflating open-cell foam enclosed in a nylon waterproof case is best (Therm-a-Rest or other brands). Unless you're very tall, you don't need the long one; put extra packs or clothes under your feet. Closed-cell foam (blue foam, Ensolite, black foam) is also warm but offers less padding. For really uneven ground or cold weather, use your extra clothes, life jackets, whatever you've got, for extra padding.

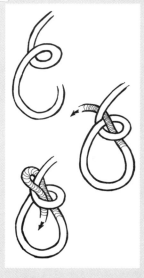

Best is to have a friend teach you some knots, but here are two that can take care of most of your needs: the rabbit (bowline) and the gopher (power cinch).

The rabbit's knot or bowline makes a loop of any size that will not jam or get smaller. You can use this to create a carrying handle that won't squash your hand or a loop to throw. Climbers use a more complex version to tie themselves into a rope; if they fall the rope loop won't tighten and crush them.

• Make a rabbit hole (like writing a 6).

• The rabbit (end of the rope) comes up out of her hole.

• She runs around the tree...

• ...and pops back down into the hole again.

• Now pull tight, holding all parts—the loop, the running end, and the "tree."

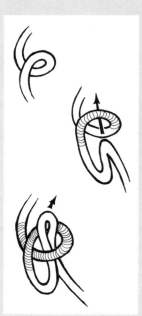

The gopher knot, or power cinch, or modified trucker's hitch (I think of it as Janet's knot, from the canoe outfitter who first showed it to me). This makes a temporary loop through which you run the end of the rope to create a pulley, enabling you to fasten a rope down *very* tight. Use this to tie tent ropes, to run a laundry line or tarp line so tight it will sing, or to fasten a canoe or gear onto a cartop.

• Make a gopher hole (same as the rabbit hole) . . .

• . . . and make a gopher underground (a loop of rope, not the end).

• The gopher peeks up out of her hole . . .

• . . . and the end of rope (which has first passed around your bumper, a cartop carrier, or a tree—whatever you are fastening the rope to) passes through the gopher's head . . .

• . . . and runs back and is tied off.

◆ A decent sleeping bag. *Not* a "four-season" bag, which is too warm
for summer, but one suited to the seasons when you usually camp.
Short women find a lot of excess space at their feet—that's extra air
for your body to try to warm up. A few manufacturers make special
short-length bags, but you can stuff extra clothes at your feet to fill
that space.

◆ A flat surface. This is the most elusive ingredient in camp beds. If
your feet are slightly downhill, prop something under them, just to
trick your body into relaxing.

◆ Dry bedwear and socks—not what you've been wearing during the
day.

◆ Perhaps a sleeping bag liner. In hot weather, a light cotton sheet; in
cool weather, a flannel sheet or bunting liner.

If you and a regular bed partner are also camping partners,
definitely get bags with compatible zippers—much warmer and nicer.
A good combination is one down bag for on top (light and fluffy) and
a synthetic bag for underneath (it compresses less).

The Tent

Do you even need a tent? Well, yes, in bug country or rain or snow
you do, but when there are none of these to keep out, at least consider
pitching your tent just in case, but sleeping under the stars. You'll hear
the night sounds better, and your mind will travel farther. Less snoring
nearby, too. Tents are the glory of modern camping gear, many
exquisitely made, and of great variety. If you're just beginning, you
don't need a bombproof, expensive mountain tent. On the other hand,
unless you're only planning on car camping, avoid high-walled family-
size tents. Definitely avoid those discount store, single-wall pup tents
(miserably hot, and moisture condenses—this could squelch your
enthusiasm fast). Get a good freestanding tent of lightweight
breathable nylon with separate rain fly, either a dome shape or some
general A-frame type. I like tents with vestibules, for stashing my pack
and boots. I also like two doorways, for peaceful coexistence with my
tent partner and for security. (When the tent gets old, if one zipper
fails in insect country, you can duct-tape it shut and use the other.)

Unless a trip requires ultralight packing and therefore maximum
use of tent space, I like to use a "four-man" tent for two or three
people, or suggest people bring tents so small they don't have to share
them. The older the group of women, the more everyone values
space, privacy, and quiet.

Other Camp Furniture

The tarp. A tent may be optional, but in rain or hot sun nothing provides more comfort than a tarp. Get a good-size one, of lightweight nylon; if it doesn't have a lot of grommets and tie-points, add some so you can pitch it a variety of ways. Where there are no handy trees to pitch it to, I carry some spare tent pole sections. (A tarp doubles as a canoe sail, a signal device, and a catcher of rain for drinking water.)

The sit-upon. If you're insulated from the damp and cold, you'll spend more time wildlife watching, photography, and the like. As Brownie Scouts we constructed "sit-upons" as our very first bit of camping gear—layers of newspaper covered with oilcloth and stitched up with green yarn. These days it's simpler to cut a square of closed-cell foam. (When you aren't sitting on it, it doubles as padding in your backpack and insulates your stove from the cold.) A few years ago some cunning folks took this idea a step farther, sewing a bright nylon case for two squares of foam, adding straps and buckles—voilà, a folding chair with a back! Crazy Creek and other companies sold millions of them. "Decadent!" we sneered, but now I'd hardly go camping without one. (These double as extra insulation under your sleeping bag, and I've seen them worn as rain hats.)

Chairs with legs. Now we're talking real luxury and heresy. Purists scorn them, but when you're car camping or even on some canoe trips, bring a short-legged beach or canvas chair and you could get wealthy renting it out. Friends who canoed the entire Yukon were a little embarrassed about bringing small beach chairs until they met an Alaska woman, paddling the river alone, with a full-size lawn recliner. Older women really appreciate the comfort. I don't actually bring chairs myself (maybe I can't think of a second use), but I'm advocating open-mindedness.

Now Leave Home!

Your cozy camp is arranged—now get out of it. If your main goal were comfort, you could have stayed home and watched nature programs on TV. Don't get so obsessed with gear, skills, and chores that you forget why you came. Look for animal tracks, notice plants, go for a midnight walk. If previous campers have left their sign, pack up their litter in your extra garbage bag, and then (unless you're in fragile alpine meadows or other areas where you shouldn't leave the trail) go ramble around.

For Further Reading

There are vast numbers of books on camping skills; the most useful will be those specific to your ways of travel and your geographic area. Books on skills relevant to specific kinds of travel—backpacking, canoeing, and so on—are included in chapters 9 and 10. See the appendix for sources of more camping skills books and guidebooks. Minimum-impact camping techniqes also vary with the terrain; a good introduction is Michael Hodgson's *The Basic Essentials™ of Minimizing Impact on the Wilderness* (Guilford, Conn.: The Globe Pequot Press, 1991).

Outdoor Cooking, Cuisine to Grub

*See that for your camping trip is provided a man cook....
Dear woman who goes hunting with her husband, be sure
that you have it understood that you do no cooking, or
dishwashing. I think that the reason women so often dislike
camping out is because the only really disagreeable part of it
is left to them as a matter of course.*

—Grace Gallatin Seton, *A Woman Tenderfoot*, 1900

New Cooking Habits

Meals are often a high point of a day on the trail. If you're a creative cook at home, you can have a great time improvising and inventing improbable campfire dishes. (Creampuffs? Nori rolls?) Adding a few wild greens for garnish earns you many points. Even if you have no kitchen confidence, you can be sure that just about anything you cook outside will be eaten with enthusiasm. Some people even love dishwashing outdoors, having established the tradition that someone reads to the dishwasher or gives her a neck rub. But Grace Seton is right about one thing: Cooking gets really disagreeable if people just assume it's your job. If you're the head cook at home and go camping with your family, establish new patterns right away. Men are supposed to barbecue, right? If you have the kids along, make the food so simple they can cook it. Rotate shifts; if you use open fires, make cook and fire tender two separate jobs. Cooks *never* wash dishes.

Campers get very attached to their own ways of doing things, including cooking, so you're likely to hear a lot of rules. But really, almost anything goes in outdoor cookery. All extremes are possible. Some get every meal out of a foil package; others wouldn't touch freeze-dried food. You *don't* need specialized camping food, freeze-dried food, breakfasts that look like breakfast, hot lunches, or fresh (or dried) meat. Get an outdoor cookbook for new menu ideas, but for the most part, just shop at your usual markets and let your outdoor meals be a variation on how you usually cook, simplified. Substitute dry ingredients for fresh, omit some things, precook parts of the dinner, cook in one pot rather than several stages. For a short trip you can precook meals and freeze them.

All Extremes Are Possible, Not Desirable

One canoe trip leader in our part of the country always brings along a full set of cast-iron pots for multicourse gourmet meals. People grumble about carrying them. On the other hand, several of my friends decided one year that we Americans pay altogether too much attention to food. For a monthlong trip they packed the same hot cereal for every breakfast, since they didn't like hot cereal anyway, and for every dinner they simply made variations on brown rice. What happened? They got so bored with the meals that they obsessed about food constantly.

Meals to Try

◆ Simple, almost no-cook food (especially in hot weather or when traveling alone): peanut butter, almond butter, fruit and nuts, instant soups, beef jerky.

◆ Ethnic foods (a good way to find tasty non-red-meat meals): burritos and tostadas; Middle Eastern pocket bread; falafels and nutburgers (mixes are available in the health food section of the supermarket); Asian noodles and soups.

◆ Foods of the area you are traveling in: for Florida, a camper's simpli-fied version of Key lime pie; Mexican food in Baja; wild rice in the northern canoe country.

◆ Old family recipes, or old-time cooking.

◆ Nostalgia food. Childhood recipes from going to camp. (Don't be disappointed, though, if S'Mores, Angels on Horseback, or M & Ms stirred into vanilla pudding aren't a big hit with people who didn't go to your camp.)

◆ Comfort foods: pastas, instant mashed potatoes.

◆ Any one-pot stews and casseroles.

The only real rules should be that meals are substantial, fairly easy to fix, not subject to spoiling, and carefully packed. Have an extra soup or two in case of delay. Bring a surprise treat to pull out on a rainy day. Pack enough chocolate and coffee and all will be well.

Packing the Food

Camp cooking is a breeze—it's the *packing* that's most of the work. Just about everything needs to be repackaged to save space, to avoid breakage, or to create convenience on the trail. No glass bottles, just high-quality plastic ones. Coffee or powdered milk will mess up the zip on a zipper-lock bag pretty fast, so use another bag inside. Avoid using twist-ties on bags (they will escape and litter the landscape); instead use rubber bands, or just tie bags shut. (Tie them *loosely!*) If you must have fresh eggs, wrap each one in its own plastic bag, and pack them all inside an old coffee can surrounded by flour, oatmeal, or the like. You get the idea—any food that can escape its package, will. Pack the plastic bags inside cloth sacks to confine it all. Heat-sealed bags are a good precaution, but I've never bothered unless I'm packing for several weeks on a river.

If you're new to camp cooking or want meals to be as efficient and simple as possible, pack everything you need for a meal together in one bag, with all directions clearly printed so anyone can cook it. (One exception is that anything to be kept cool—butter, cheese, chocolate—might go together, to be kept deep in a pack out of the sun or perhaps stowed in a denim sack to be wet down and kept cool by evaporation.) On the other hand, when experienced campers or experienced cooks travel together, leave some room for creativity and improvising. The main dishes can be prepackaged, but include a big sack of soup fixings, dessert ingredients, baking supplies, or—if you plan to catch fish—spices or makings for chowder.

Kitchen Apparatus

Get better-than-average camp pots and pans. Standard camp kits are aluminum, which heats up quickly but is often so thin that food burns easily. Anyway, you may object to aluminum in your diet. Get a set of nested stainless-steel kettles. Enamelware is another possibility, but it's hard to find enamel kettles that nest well. Most camp frying pans are too thin to be useful. If weight isn't a concern, use cast iron; if it is, use a pan with a nonstick surface. A good utensil kit is any cloth roll with pockets for a long-handled spatula, a rubber scraper, a tiny little whisk, a tiny little grater, a can opener, and so on. Surplus stores sometimes have them, or you can sew your own. Spices can be packed in 35 mm film cans.

Baking on the Trail

Tottery aluminum reflector ovens are pretty obsolete; they've been replaced by Dutch-oven baking, to the grief of reflector-oven loyalists. A Dutch oven is just a covered pot you can put in the ashes, heaping coals on top. There are lightweight models made for camping, or you can improvise with a flat lid on a tall frying pan. A great way to fix gingerbread, quick breads, cinnamon rolls. I once heard a rather self-important trip leader mention "Dutch-Oven Theory," but really the only secret to Dutch-oven baking is to put *plenty* of coals or even a twig fire on the lid, and take great care not to have too much heat underneath—don't put the pan right onto coals, prop it up over them.

Cinnamon rolls on the tundra.

Dishwashing

One standard practice for keeping kettles clean has been to coat the bottom and sides with liquid soap. Bad idea: It introduces a lot of potentially polluting soap into the environment, and if any soap gets *inside* the pot, it can cause camper's runs just as effectively as bacteria. Cook on a stove and pots stay pretty clean. If you use open fires, you could just decide that black is a beautiful color for camping pots. Children's camps often make a fetish of scrubbing off all soot until the kettles shine. Surely adult women have better things to do. Let the black build up, I say, and nest your kettles with plastic bags between them. No soap or food-contaminated water goes into any lake or river, of course. In fact, you rarely need soap; sand and a scrubbie do a fine job.

Resources

FOR FURTHER READING: COOKBOOKS

No one book defines cookery; use several cookbooks, to avoid boredom. For simplicity I used the same cookbook for years—until one day, stirring a cooking pot on a wilderness river, I knew that hungry as I was, I could never again eat even one spoonful of mung bean stew. Ditto the lentil chili. And I have not. Here's a wide variety of cookbooks, most of which have stood the test of time.

Fleming, June. *The Well-Fed Backpacker.* 1976. Reprint, New York: Vintage Books, 1986. Based on supermarket ingredients.

Jacobson, Cliff. *Basic Essentials™: Cooking in the Outdoors.* 2d ed. Old Guilford, Conn.: The Globe Pequot Press, 1999.

Latimer, Carole. *Wilderness Cuisine: How to Prepare and Enjoy Fine Food on the Trail and in Camp.* Berkeley: Wilderness Press, 1991. The recipes look pretty high tone for camp use, but every one I've tried is worth the trouble, and much of the preparation is at home, before the trip.

McHugh, Gretchen. *The Hungry Hiker's Book of Good Cooking.* 1984. Reprint, New York: Knopf, 1996. Includes information on drying your own food and using camp stoves.

Miller, Dorcas. *Good Food for Camp and Trail: All-Natural Recipes for Delicious Meals Outdoors.* Boulder: Pruett Publishing, 1993.

Safety, Health, and Beauty

We were told that we looked terrible. We knew that and demanded something to eat. Then there was a lot of business with soap and hot water, to make us feel equal to those large soft beds. . . . "Doesn't that feel good? After sleeping on the ground for so long!" We did not wish to be impolite, but we were hot and restless the whole night, feeling stuffy.

—Anna Kalland, "It Can't Be Done," *Outing* magazine, 1923

Let's take these concerns in reverse order, partly because many safety concerns are beyond the scope of this book, and partly because some general beauty-hygiene-tidiness concerns do have significant impact on camping life.

Many years ago a little booklet, supposedly meant to encourage women, devoted way too many pages to assuring the reader that beauty need not suffer in outdoor life. Some of the advice was pretty silly: Carry those extra sandals and shorts to assure him, your very own Robert Redford, "Yes, indeed, you are a woman"; wear bee pollen perfume. [Oh, no, not in mosquito country!] The author's advice on taking a sponge bath is almost prurient: A noise! You leap behind a rock! "What if a deer should see you? Would it notice you are naked?" ("Would it *care*?" we would chorus.) It was, for a time, our campfire amusement to do dramatic readings—quite dramatic—from this book, which we referred to as "The Total (Woods)Woman."

I certainly have no wish to revive all that anxiety about whether one can be "feminine" and still a hardcore camper. Nor any expertise on it. But, let's face it, a lot of perfectly nice women are put off by the notion popular in some circles that one is supposed to come home from camping unwashed, unshaven, and ripe smelling. "Roughing it," you know. Do you have to get so grody?

Washing Up

There are a few women who after a week on the trail still look more uptown than I ever manage. It's a recessive gene for repelling dirt, I think. The rest of us, depending on our level of fastidiousness and our circumstances, can try these things:

◆ If you just have to have a shower every day and aren't comfortable away from modern plumbing, you'll have to stick to day trips or find parks that have all the amenities. (But think about how much compulsive showering depletes an area's water resources, and at least get in the habit of turning the water off while you soap up.)

◆ Around water (not fragile desert potholes!), try the ritual of a swim or quick dip every day, no matter how cold the water. You'll be glad later. (My personal record is thirty-three degrees, for seven seconds. Was it was worth it?)

◆ Pack a nice towel, if you must, or use just a bandanna. Better yet, buy a super-absorbent "sport-sponge" to avoid carrying around a damp towel.

◆ You really can do a sponge bath with about a ½ cup of water, as polar travelers do.

◆ Carry premoistened travel towels when you're around salt water, or in cold conditions.

◆ When you can't wash your clothes, air them whenever possible in sun and wind.

◆ Whatever methods of washing you use, *no soap* (not even biodegradable) goes into the water. Pour all soapy water out well back from any lakes or streams.

◆ On women's trips we sometimes make a big production, a celebration, out of cleaning up, especially when it's been difficult. One way is to rig a steam bath: Wrap a tarp or plastic sheet over a tent frame. Heat rocks (not rocks that have been under water) in a fire outside the tent, and carry them into the shelter in a pot or with forked sticks. Sprinkle water on them very sparingly.

As a trip comes to an end, don't let things run down, as you think of home and washing in real hot water. Try to keep yourself and your gear in good shape, prepared to go on for several more days. I'm not sure why this seems important; I think it's about really making the outdoors your home.

Natural bathing—no soap, of course!

Hair Washing

Hair washing is a great morale booster. Camping once in a drizzly Alaska bog, we spent half a day at it. We heated water on the stove. We rinsed each other's hair, trying to pose like women on Grecian urns. Someone set up a haircutting station, with beauty-parlor gossip. In case you ever need to know, it is possible to give a reasonable haircut with the scissors of a Swiss army knife.

Okay, I'll be honest. Sooner or later there will come a time when your hands are covered with permadirt, you have greasy hat hair, and your only clean clothes are out in the rain. When getting clean demands time, energy, or resources that just are not available, be philosophical. At least it's honest dirt, not smog and toxic wastes. And you won't keep getting infinitely grubbier. New dirt wears off old, or, as a scientist with long months of field work explained, "You come to dynamic equilibrium with your own dirt." Assume your inner beauty is showing through—if you're happy, it probably is.

Some Useful Potions

Some women bring little more than a toothbrush. One woman sneaked a butane hair curler along on a remote wilderness river. ("Way to go!" we said, when we discovered it.) Here are a few critical items:

◆ Unscented soaps and shampoo or those scents that are unappealing to bugs, like citronella, pine tar, rosemary, eucalyptus, peppermint.

◆ Skin moisturizers, any time of year. A good sunscreen. Aloe vera or other after-sun, after-wind creams.

◆ Hand cream—the heavy-duty, industrial-strength kind. Very cold weather demands drastic measures to keep fingers from developing painful cracks. An Arctic airplane mechanic told me he soaks his hands in #30 motor oil! Pure lanolin, greasy as it is, is better. Many of us prefer Bag Balm, the stuff you buy at a farm supply store (and a few discriminating drugstores). Carrying a little jar of cold sore ointment around in your pocket also works well for your hands, and you'll remember to use it often.

◆ Lip ointments that contain sunscreen. On the water or on bright snow, it's easy to get a painful sunburn on your lower lip. I've let it happen an embarrassing number of times. My friend Pam, looking at my Victorian lady "bee-stung" pout, had good advice: "I carry *five* Chapsticks. In my pants pocket, my jacket pocket, my day pack, my tent pocket, and a little pocket I sewed onto my sleeping bag for Kleenex." The truly Chapstick-dependent hang it around their necks.

Your Period

Your period may come early, especially if you go on a long trip with other women. Those pheromones do kick in, and you'll get in synch, so carry supplies. Small tampons are the handiest, but if you bring some pads, too, they double as emergency compresses to augment your first-aid kit. What do you do with the used tampons and pads? Burn them, when it's safe. (This will take a *really* hot fire.) Better yet, carry them out. (Pack along little plastic bags; put a used tea bag or crushed aspirin in with them, they say, to reduce the odor.) *Don't bury them.* Your pet dogs love to raid bathroom wastebaskets; wild animals, too, will be curious and dig them up.

Bears and you. This brings us to the urgent question I've been asked so often: Is it dangerous for a woman with her period to be in bear country? No more than for anyone else. Most people's fears are unnecessary, since 99-plus percent of the bears campers meet are black bears (even though some may be brown in color). Black bears aren't in the habit of attacking people. Attacks have occurred, infrequently, but an unprovoked and serious black bear attack is abnormal. (There *are* sociopath bears—but on the whole bears have a lot better behavior record than humans.) What interests black bears is your food, not you, so avoid bear hassles by keeping a clean camp and keeping food odors down.

Brown bears, or grizzlies (now found only in a few parts of the Rockies, and in western Canada and Alaska), are another story. They are by nature aggressive and can be dangerous to our species. (Polar bears are even more so, but camping out in polar bear country is way past Basic Essentials.) They are most dangerous when they're familiar with humans and crowded, as in Yellowstone. If you camp in bear country, you owe it to yourself to learn all you can about their habits, how to avoid them, and what to do if attacked. But if you're a woman between adolescence and menopause, don't get into special bear paranoia. There is *no evidence* that menstruation has anything at all to do with the serious, but infrequent, brown bear attacks. (You'll see warnings in a few National Park Service pamphlets—in a culture so prone to lawsuits, they probably have to cover themselves.) Actually, many human odors are known to *attract* bears—sexual odors, perfumes, toothpaste, interesting human food. But often we don't know what made a specific bear *attack*. In other words, *everyone* who enters the territory of brown bears should be respectful of their power, stay out of their way, and learn good bear manners.

Other Body Processes

Drink enough water. It's crucial to staying healthy outdoors (or in the city). Coffee and tea don't count. Being dehydrated makes you cranky and irritable, and contributes to headaches, bad judgment, hypothermia, and constipation. It makes worse any other health or injury problem. If you don't urinate for hours, don't be pleased at the convenience—it's dangerous. If your urine is intensely colored (pay attention to this), you need to drink more. You can't rely on finding uncontaminated water sources; you need to carry water, boil it, filter it, or treat it. Especially when it's cold, it's easy to forget to drink. You can't count on thirst for a cue; fill your water bottle and be sure it's all gone on schedule.

When you do drink enough, the natural consequences are a little more inconvenient for women than for men. This is really a very minor problem, although it's amusing that it has been raised as an obstacle to having women on expeditions: "But what about excretory situations?" men have asked. The solution is obvious: Other people can turn their backs. You can improvise a "widdling tin" for the tent at night (old coffee cans are good; zipper-lock bags are for experts only). Ingenious manufacturers have worried about this matter enough to invent little funnel devices so that we, too, can urinate standing up. I'll confess I haven't tried them, and I don't even know anyone who has. A health survey taken among women in cold-weather strenuous sports reported almost no use of them. A lighthearted "equipment review" in *Women Outdoors* magazine pointed out that some leak because of poor fit, and the disposable kind create another potential litter problem.

While we're on indelicate subjects, let's consider digestive irregularities. Change of activity, water, and diet often cause mild constipation or looseness. Treat the former by drinking more and eating more bulky food, or prunes, or fresh berries and greens. Treat the latter by avoiding solid food if necessary (lots of water, though!), then starting on crackers. Treat your digestion with diet before even considering drastic first-aid measures. One common reason for the runs is not infection but overzealous soaping of the dishwater with inadequate rinsing. Giardiasis (a main reason for filtering water) can be a serious disturbance, but it usually won't hit you until you're back home.

A trivial camping question that seems to bother people is: "How much toilet paper shall I bring?" One correct answer is none, since natural substitutes are available. Here's another correct answer, one many people prefer: Bring enough to make people comfortable, but use as little as possible, and leave *none* behind. Tuck part of a roll and several little plastic bags in your day pack. Burn toilet paper at the cat hole where you use it only if that is absolutely safe. Or burn it in the campfire. Or pack it out. Do *not* bury it. The natural organic matter you leave behind will, if disposed of properly ("properly" varies with the terrain), decompose from the action of soil microbes or sun. Toilet paper lasts too long, a disgusting reminder of some people's weirdness: too squeamish not to use paper, but not a bit reluctant to ornament the landscape with it.

Before You Go

Use a trip to wild country as an occasion to do health-related things you should have done anyway—get that tooth fixed, get a spare pair of glasses. Check with your doctor about specific concerns. (People with diabetes, for example, will almost certainly find some changes in their chemical balance.) If you are going on an organized trip, and are asked to fill out a medical information form, do it completely and honestly. In more than twenty years of guiding, I've seen very few potentially dangerous situations, but two of them occurred only because people lied on their medical forms.

Avoiding Injury

Women have several assets here. We generally pay attention to our bodies; we're willing to ask for help; we aren't likely to try to prove ourselves through showing off or recklessness. Aside from learning to perform physical motions correctly and practicing common sense, the best accident prevention is knowing your limits and stopping in time. Avoid many minor sprains and strains and sore muscles by stretching. Do it when you get up, before lifting or hard walking, and at the end of a day to get kinks out. Late in the day is when people get careless, through tiredness or hurry; watch out for the Home Free Phenomenon.

Getting in Shape

Well, yes, do it, of course. But don't wait until some mythical time of better fitness to start having fun outdoors. The body you have now, whatever shape it's in, is ready to go. Women who've called themselves "marshmallowy but resilient," or who have warned me, "My enthusiasm for this trip is exceeded only by my flab," have had a wonderful time. It's true, of course, that you'll enjoy physical activities more if you're really conditioned for them, but the best training is usually doing them. Once you're having fun, the motivation to get in shape will probably follow.

Resources

FOR FURTHER READING

Everyone, women and men, should have basic knowledge of first aid—for camping or for city life, where accidents are more likely. Red Cross training is widely available. These courses are based on the assumption that medical aid is as close as 911, so sooner or later you'll want to take some classes specifically designed for wilderness first aid.

Good reference books for a lay audience are:

Forgey, William W., M.D. *Basic Essentials™: Wilderness First Aid.* 2d ed. Guilford, Conn.: The Globe Pequot Press, 1999.

Isaac, Jeffrey. *The Outward Bound Wilderness First-Aid Handbook.* New York: The Lyons Press, 1998.

James A. Wilkerson, ed. *Medicine for Mountaineering.* 3d ed. Seattle: The Mountaineers, 1985.

For further information on an essential aspect of hygiene:

Meyer, Kathleen. *How to Shit in the Woods.* Berkeley: Ten Speed Press, 1989. There's a special chapter for women in this explicit, very funny book, and the author's advice is sage and environmentally sound.

Dressing for Success in the Bush

No woman knows, until she tries it, what a relief it is to travel in the woods without a skirt and without big baggy bloomers to catch on everything.

—Rena Phillips, "A Woman on the Trail," *Outing* magazine, 1904

From Corsets to Gore-Tex: The Evolution of Camping Clothes

In our great-grandmothers' day, a woman—that is, a *lady*—who liked outdoor adventure had a real problem with clothes. (Women who routinely lived and *worked* outdoors were a bit less oppressed by fashion.) Trousers were too "dreadful" to consider, and ladylike garments weren't made for action. In 1901 mountaineer Annie Peck warned women how dangerous it was to wear corsets for climbing; the same year a free-spirited canoeist advised women to "leave behind the trammels of conventionality"—but the "trammels" she meant were just "whalebone stays and patent leather slippers." Long skirts were still de rigeur.

Gradually, however, the bolder women, once they got out of sight of towns, started taking off their skirts, under which they were sneakily wearing boys' knickers. Next came the scandalous bloomers, introduced by bicyclists, who didn't want yards of material catching in their spokes. Fisherwomen started wearing riding jodhpurs. Freedom of movement was being won, very slowly. Still, even encumbered by their impractical outfits, these women made some very impressive journeys.

Come to think of it, we wore some pretty silly camping clothes when I started camping. Perky little sailor hats, with no brim to keep

A canoeist, 1889.

off sun or rain. Blue jeans, which stayed wet for days. Hooded sweatshirts, which acted like sponges. We were wet and cold a lot, but we had great fun, and many of us got hooked on camping for life. The next period was dominated by army surplus gear. Women's sizes weren't easy to find, but what great stuff! Tightly woven wool gabardine pants. Norwegian army pants with an extra layer on the seat and knees. "Jungle pants" with cargo pockets big enough to lose your binoculars and bird book in, ankle strings to keep out insects, and a lot of other little tabs and cords that I never have figured out. Most surplus store outfits were pretty funky, but what do serious campers care about fashion?

Then, suddenly, camping was In. Everybody started manufacturing women's outdoor clothes, first in wonderful earth tones, then in berry colors, then in lemon, purple, and hot pink. These days you can pick your outdoor image: Ms. Rambo in army surplus. Out of Africa in tastefully rumpled khaki. Or fashion queen, every petroleum-based garment color coordinated.

One lesson of all this? Wear what makes you comfortable and happy. Thoreau cautioned us, "Beware of all enterprises that require new clothes."

It *Looks* Like Good Outdoor Clothing. Is It?

Watch out for impostors, clothes made for the Outdoor Look, not for outdoor life. Inferior faux-camping clothes now have the same problems we used to complain about back before they made outdoor clothing for women:

◆ Not enough pockets in women's pants. (Can't spoil the fanny line!)

◆ Women's clothing sometimes isn't stitched strongly.

◆ Clothes that look good are cut too tight for real action.

◆ Shirts and jackets are cut too tight for many women's hips.

A Brief Consumer's Guide to Materials and Layers

There are two rules for good camping clothes: Buy the right materials for your use; combine several layers for good protection.

Cotton is a mixed blessing. It grows in Dixie––use it in hot weather. It breathes well and it cools you down. Soak your cotton hat or bandanna to cool your body and temper. Cotton T-shirts for summer. Long-sleeved, lightweight cotton shirts to keep off sunburn and mosquitoes.

Do *not* wear cotton in wet or cold weather. Winter campers put it concisely: *Cotton kills!* It gets damp easily, stays damp, and cools you right down. (Wet denim sacks from your cutoff jeans are good "refrigerators" for butter and cheese in hot weather.) Some winter underwear is cotton, or a cotton blend. Don't buy it, or wear it only after skiing, sipping brandy by the fireplace. Don't wear cotton socks when your feet will be in and out of water all day (fish-belly feet!). Above all, *don't wear blue jeans for camping.* Sure, you see denim on campers everywhere, on the Marlboro man, and on Inuit boys by icy Alaska rivers. That's just marketing.

A substitute for cotton. Supplex nylon has the soft, comfortable drape of cotton and makes good warm-weather shirts and pants, but has the virtue of drying very quickly.

Wool retains warmth even when wet. Loosely woven, wool contains many dead-air spaces for insulation; tightly woven, it has great wind resistance. Wool was crucial for jackets and shirts, hats, gloves, and socks. Now you can choose between wool and synthetics. Wool long johns are obsolete. But if you find part-angora long johns, snap them up! They've about disappeared from the earth, except for one company in Germany.

Synthetics are great for warmth and wicking. Once upon a time there was just "pile"—a bulky petroleum product that substituted for wool, dried fast, and wore well. Then new softer, thinner, nicer-looking fabrics arrived: bunting, Synchilla, Capilene, Thermax, Thermolactyl, and many other newer proprietary names (I'm probably a few years' behind). There are light, soft synthetics for underwear and heavier weaves for jackets and insulation. They retain warmth when wet and wick moisture away from your skin at least as well as wool. They dry faster. Especially useful: lightweight liner socks to wear inside wool socks, and long underwear for skiing and other perspiration-producing activities.

Wool versus Synthetics: A Matter of Personal Preference

- ◆ Feel: Wool might make you itch; some synthetics feel about as cozy as plastic.
- ◆ Care: Wool shrinks. Some synthetics shrink down to doll clothes in the dryer, or melt over the campfire.
- ◆ Smell: Wet wool doesn't smell great. Neither do some synthetics when combined with particular people's perspiration.
- ◆ Aethetics, tradition, sentiment, whim.

Fur and feathers. Birds and beasts are dressed just right for their climates. Humans don't have very good pelts, so we steal, killing the original owners. Most antifur protests focus on the questionable ethics of fur farming and killing for luxury and status. People who live in severe climates use furs for better reasons: Wolverine parka ruffs prevent frostbite; beaver mittens keep a sled-dog driver's hands from freezing. Humans could not have survived in polar regions without the furs and meat of animals. Animal lives are also lost for some of the other best clothing materials we have: goosedown, leather, sheepskin. And synthetics use up nonrenewable petroleum resources. Face it, there aren't many pure, low-impact clothes.

Gore-Tex and other rainwear materials. Nylon, in various weaves, is very tough and used in windproof garments, as well as (coated) for rainwear. The problem is that in waterproof fabrics, you can perspire so much you get wetter from inside than from the rain. Gore-Tex (and other companies' newer proprietary fabrics) was invented to be tough and waterproof and to breathe, making excellent rainwear for active sports. It is wonderful as a windbreaker; it gets mixed reviews on its waterproof qualities in extreme (or dirty) conditions.

Your Rain Gear

This could be your most important purchase. There are several choices:

◆ Use Gore-Tex or other breathable fabrics when sweating really matters (backpacking, for instance). Expensive.

◆ Coated nylon has many uses; much less expensive.

◆ Plastic ponchos or rainsuits. Cheap. Not worth it; they'll tear right away.

◆ For extreme wet, when sweating isn't an issue, rubberized sailor's foul-weather gear is best; relatively expensive.

Whatever type you choose, get a complete suit of rain jacket and pants, and get them roomy. If you have long hair, watch out for Velcro fasteners at the neck. Sometimes a rain poncho is sufficient; they are nice and cool, and can cover your backpack, but it's hard to both be very active and stay dry inside one.

Plastic. It has its uses. Plastic bags, for emergency use. I often have a couple of big leaf bags tucked into a pocket or day pack. Cut holes for your head and arms, and it's a pretty good emergency rain tunic. On a monthlong trip in Alaska, two women got along pretty well on Hefty bags when their expensive new rain gear failed. If a sudden cold rain soaks your clothing, you can wear a plastic bag *inside* your clothes, as a vapor barrier (keeping your warm body moisture from leaving). Not comfortable, but good hypothermia prevention. Smaller strong bags make good emergency liners when your boots get soaked. If your socks are wet, too, wring them out, and wear the bags inside. One rainy October day a woman wearing bread bags on both feet, with matching daisies around the ankles, claimed, "Learning about this was worth the whole cost of the trip." Save every bag you packed food in, and always stash a few extras in your pack or pocket.

A mother and daughter in matching garbage bags.

The Layered Look

The first layer is a second skin, which helps wick body moisture away from you; next come insulation layers, holding warm air; the outer layer is your shell, which keeps you and your insulation safe from wind and rain. Your garments should all be cut loosely enough to allow for proper layering, and easily removable to encourage you to add and subtract layers often. (Before you are too warm, or too cold!) Front zippers are often preferable to pullovers for this reason. A dickey or scarf instead of a turtleneck keeps you from overheating. Your hat is your best thermal regulator: When your feet are cold, put a hat on; take it off to avoid sweating up your clothes. A little day pack or fanny pack to stow the extra clothes in is handy.

Footwear

Walking and backpacking. Remember those heavy "waffle-stomper" boots, the hefty ones with red laces that people used to trudge to college classes in? Out, these days. For most purposes light boots (all-leather or leather and fabric) are easier on you and on the earth.

Around water and in camp. Sport sandals are a great recent invention. Teva and Alp make tough ones with Velcro straps, or try the "apostle style" with lots of wraparound thongs. Most all-canvas boots don't hold up well at all.

Around cold water. Neoprene wet-suit booties are good for a few hours at a time, but if you wear them all day for too many days, you may develop painful trench foot. A newer development is Gore-Tex socks. For longer wear use knee-high rubber boots with a lot of wool socks and a wool felt insole. (Red Ball boots come in women's sizes.)

Very cold weather. Boots will be cold if they are too snug for two pairs of socks and you can't wiggle your feet. Rubber bottoms are cold. For extremes, use boots with built-in insulation (army "Mickey Mouse" or Korean boots, LaCrosse Iceman boots). Real luxury is mukluks. You can get lined coated nylon ones to be worn over running shoes, or soft leather and canvas ones with felt or wool liners.

Some Finicky Thoughts on Fabric and Color

Visual pollution. Some campers will consider your loud "artificial" colors an intrusion. As environmental concerns go, this is very small potatoes. The animals don't care, or even notice, if you wear hot pink. However, for blending in when you want to get close to animals, wear camouflage or soft plaids, not solid colors.

Photography. Bright "National Geographic red" is the cliché contrast spot against blue and green. Subtle earth tones and deep reds harmonize well. Orange, purple, and the like could look hot and exciting, or just jarring.

Insect attraction. No one agrees on *exactly* which colors work, but in general mosquitoes love blue and most deep, rich colors. They are bored by white or tan. Some gnats and flies will swarm all over particular shades of orange, bright yellow, or red.

Safety. Life jackets are good in red or yellow; if you dare be in the woods during hunting season, orange, scarlet, or pink are the colors of choice. On the other hand, many women who camp alone or in small groups in heavily traveled areas prefer to be very inconspicuous.

Noise. Nylon, Gore-Tex and some other synthetics rustle a lot. If you want to move silently, not spooking animals, wear soft natural fabrics.

The Real World—Notes from the Field

Experienced campers have fun with outdoor clothes and break our own rules. I often go snowshoeing in jeans. Edith goes canoeing wearing— against advice—bib-top overalls she calls "hogwashers" and a straw hat. Kristin favors dashing wide-brimmed black desperado hats with a feather. Marsha loves wild Hawaiian shirts. When she's guiding, she doesn't wear them on the first day ("I guess it wouldn't help my credibility, would it?"), but by day three the wild clothes come out. If you can't escape the tyranny of fashion on a camping trip, when can you?

Part III:

Traveling without Wheels: Skills and Styles

Water Travels

The innate rhythm of the canoe is in you somewhere and the two come together in a great harmony. It is only for you to follow the lead of instinct, the greatest thing in the world, as any animal will tell you.

—Leslie Glendower Peabody,
"The Canoe and the Woman," *Outing* magazine, 1901

Canoeing gets more attention in this book than any other activity—not only because it's my own passion and expertise, but also as a way to look at one sport in detail, for examples of how women learn, what we like, and the (unnecessary) obstacles that can come up in any outdoor activity.

Canoeing has grown as a popular family activity ever since the introduction of affordable and durable aluminum canoes (built from alloys developed for World War II aircraft). It's practiced casually by many people, often very badly; it's practiced with expertise and intensity in many different styles: long expeditions, whitewater, "freestyle." In recent years it has become more specialized and high-tech in gear, technique, and instruction ("canoesport," some try to call it), but canoes still have an aura of tradition, the craft in which our continent was explored.

We canoewomen are fanatic in our enthusiasm; "the very poetry of travel," gushed one of our foremothers. But I've also met many women whose previous experiences in a canoe have been very unpoetic. Canoeing (like many outdoor activities) offers rich possibilities for having a rotten time: perceived danger, heavy gear to manage, opportunities for being yelled at or feeling silly or getting frustrated, chances to be tired and miserable. Not to mention the lack of skill and instruction. This chapter is a case study in avoiding some of these problems.

How Not to Canoe

Here's an actual canoe scene, unfortunately fairly typical: A large party of young people started out from a canoe outfitter's, wearing cutoffs, T-shirts, and halter tops. There was no sign of spare clothes in their canoes, just coolers and six-packs. Watching them was a group of women leaders-in-training; we were wearing light wool, in deference to the changeable spring weather. The outfitter offered no advice or instruction, and the kids didn't ask any questions. The rented paddles, besides being very heavy, were too long for many of them. A young man jumped into the stern of each canoe, and a young woman sat in the bow; we predicted (correctly) that at the end of the day they'd all be in the same positions. As they maneuvered down the channel toward the Flambeau River, everyone was switching paddling sides pretty much at random; at some point in *all ten canoes* (we were betting on this), both partners were splashing around on the same side. Before the first river bend they were already nagging at each other, frustrated because the canoes didn't go straight. *How many things can possibly be wrong with this picture?*

We thought of the small rapids waiting ahead and one woman said emphatically, "No body heat!" (That's our shorthand for, "We'll fish these folks out of the river if necessary, but if you think I'd get in a sleeping bag with a hypothermic fool, forget it!") The ten young women especially had a potentially bad day coming up. They weren't going to get a chance to try steering, and being up front, they wouldn't even notice the guys ineffectually "ruddering" while yelling, "Paddle harder!"

A Woman's Place: This Business of Bow and Stern

How many times have I heard women say, "Well, I've canoed for several years, but only in the bow"? Or sometimes, "Only in the bow, *of course*," or, "I've never been *allowed* to paddle stern." (Emphasis mine.) This idea that in mixed-doubles canoeing the man is supposed to be in the stern has nothing to do with good technique or common sense. It's about status and power. People have the odd notion that a 17-foot craft with a crew of two needs a captain, and men are quick to jump into the supposed captain's seat.

Actually, having the brawnier paddler (presumably the man) in the stern can be contrary to the way casual paddling works. Here's why: A canoe paddled by two people (putting out *exactly* the same effort) does not naturally go in a straight line, as you may have noticed in frustration. It naturally veers off toward the side the bow paddler is on—*as if* the stern paddler were working harder. So having the stronger paddler in the bow can be a way of neutralizing that. The canoe goes straighter, the stern paddler wastes less energy on corrective steering, less effort is needed all around. When I explain this women say, "I get it! Brawn in the bow, brai . . . no, *finesse* in the stern." And so what if you don't know how steer? You'll get the hang of it in a few hours.

It's not that men should automatically take the bow, either. In canoe classes I often suggest that men paddle with other men, and women paddle together; people learn faster when there's a balance in size, strength, and (especially) style. Many people like to switch positions often, alternating the fun of steering with the joys of being in the bow, where you can space out and pretend you're all alone. (If one person is much heavier, rearrange gear to balance the canoe fore and aft.)

And who's really running things? Both of you. When you're just crossing a lake, most steering is from the stern. But in whitewater canoeing the bow paddler, who has a clearer view of what's ahead, initiates most moves. Skilled flatwater paddlers often use similar coordinated steering, with the more powerful paddler in the stern and the bow paddler initiating the turns. It's like dancing together on the water, and, as Mike Galt, freestyle paddler and designer of elegant canoes, likes to put it, "My lady leads."

First Steps

In any sport there are things so elementary that people often forget to mention them. Here are a few for canoeing:

How to get in and out of the canoe. This is when you are most likely to capsize. The canoe, for its own well-being and yours, should be fully supported by the water, *never* "bridging" (one end afloat and one up on shore). Watch out for people's chivalrous but misguided impulse to

Wilderness without Roles

Other outdoor activities have similar limiting roles. Back in the 1920s women mountaineers began what was rather quaintly called "manless climbing." It's not that they wanted to avoid men—it was just their only chance to get to be lead climbers on the rope. In any backcountry travel being the head map reader and navigator might be the "power position," one you want to share. (Sea kayaker Victoria Jason once had to paddle 100 miles in the wrong direction, protesting, with a man who refused to let her see the maps.) If there seem to be "women's roles," assume that the other ones are more fun, and well worth learning.

help a lady ashore by dragging the canoe half out of the water! There's a certain flair to this, like Sir Walter Raleigh spreading his cloak for the queen, but it's likely to dump you into the lake.

Which end is which? The front is the end where there's room for your feet ahead of the seat. This may seem ridiculously obvious, but nervous beginners do ask, and a friend once watched a physics professor (a man, who didn't ask) manage to wedge his body in the stern, facing the wrong way, and then complain bitterly of silly canoe design. Most older canoes are symmetrical end to end (you can sit backward on the bow seat, balancing your weight to paddle solo), but many newer ones are not; they're designed for smooth motion one way only.

How to sit in a canoe. *Don't be ladylike!* Sitting as if you were in a chair, knees primly together, is unstable—and very inefficient. (Here's how a canoe actually moves: You plant the paddle in water and pull your body up to the paddle; the canoe comes along. Clearly, the attachment of body to canoe is critical.) Instead kneel with your butt on the seat and your knees braced wide apart, or sit with legs firmly locked against the sides of the canoe, or feet braced—as much like an aquatic centaur as possible.

Learn an efficient, easy stroke. Keep your paddle quite vertical in the water. Use your large muscles (shoulders, back, stomach), not just your lower arms. Paddle on the opposite side from your partner, always. (Well, 99 and $^{44}/_{100}$ percent of the time.) You can switch simultaneously every few strokes, on a signal. This is "the Minnesota switch," first developed by racers, and it eliminates the need for much steering. Or each person can stick to his or her own side until tired—or for a few hours, or all day—with the stern paddler making corrective strokes to keep on course.

Give yourself time to learn. There you are zigzagging all over the lake, and your canoe is dropping way behind. You know switching paddle sides isn't the right way to steer, but it's the only way you know, so . . . Don't do it! It's inefficient, and it interferes with ever learning the right way. You're *supposed* to be zigzagging at first; once your body learns how the canoe moves, you can work on a straighter path. And paddle as if you know what you're doing—if you are too tentative, you won't know whether you're doing the wrong stroke or the right one too weakly. Make your mistakes with gusto, and your body will quickly learn what to do. (This applies to most other sports, too.) Once you can steer on the left side, you'll have to educate your right side separately, but the learning curve is quicker. Remember, if you aren't making any mistakes, you probably aren't learning much.

Well, those are some preliminaries, attitudes to hold on to. For actual coaching check out some of the books suggested in Resources, and/or get hands-on coaching. You'll learn faster if you can spend some time with a skilled teacher whose goal is your learning, not getting somewhere fast or showing off his or her own expertise. If your outdoor-experienced friends aren't experienced at teaching, you probably need to take charge of your own learning. Watch veteran canoeists closely to see how they do things. Ask a lot of questions. Don't feel bad about not being an instant expert, and don't put up with people yelling at you. ("Back off! Of course I'm not very good yet! I just started learning this morning!")

Lasting Partnerships and the No-Fault Divorce

On some canoe trips people keep the same partners the entire time, even for days or weeks. The advantage is that you and your partner become very predictable to each other, and may get to be quite good together. On the other hand, if you switch partners you can learn from adapting to different people and enjoy the company of more folks; relationships within the whole group will probably be smoother, too.

There's one time you *should* definitely switch partners: when frustration is high, and neither of you can figure out how to improve. Close friends, married couples, and Significant Others can be wildly incompatible as paddling partners—and it's not necessarily a sign of a bad relationship. (Though canoe coaches do fantasize about a lucrative enterprise: Intensive Couples Therapy on the River.) In any outdoor activity that involves risk, fears, frustration, and ego, it can be a lot easier (or at least politer) to team up with a stranger. Unless your purpose is to "work through your issues," take a break when things get sticky, *before* tempers build up. Try saying (agreeably, tactfully), "We're not getting our act together. Can we just switch partners for a while?"

Carrying Your Own Weight

"What exactly does this canoe weigh?" asked a tiny, trim woman from under a standard canoe that she was carrying around a waterfall—about a mile.

"Seventy-five pounds. Maybe closer to eighty with all the fittings."

"Omigod," she said, cheerfully. "That's three-fourths of my body weight!"

"No Fault!"

In a beginning whitewater class, a woman who was just "getting back on the horse" after a frightening capsize somehow teamed up with a paddler who was in a mood to let off steam and show off. A partnership from hell: Within minutes one was paralyzed with terror and the other frustrated and furious. An instructor yelled, "No-fault divorce!" No discussion, no blame. They each just were assigned more compatible partners, for that day only. It had looked like potential homicide, but the next day they actually chose each other as partners (isn't that just what women would do!), and that day their teamwork was fine.

It's called a "portage" ("porTAHGE" in Canada, but the French doesn't make it easier). One of the glories of canoeing is that you can so readily carry your craft between lakes, and one of the challenges is to do it with grace. Even if your canoeing involves no cross-country carrying, you still need to get the boat on top of your car. Here are several tips for handling the weight.

Lighter canoes. If you can afford them, canoes of Kevlar or blends of Kevlar and fiberglass can weigh hardly more than half the weight of ABS plastic, rotomolded plastic, or aluminum. Solo canoes (these are 13 to 15 feet long) are easy to handle.

A good yoke. Well-cushioned shoulder pads (set not more than 7 inches apart for most women), firmly attached to the center thwart.

Balance. Think of the *National Geographic* photos of women going to market carrying huge loads on their heads, with grace and dignity. Good posture is the key. Let the canoe ride you easily; because the weight bears straight down, it's easier to carry a seventy-five pound canoe than a fifty-five pound backpack.

Getting it overhead—with a little help from your friends. This is the crux of the problem, not carrying it. Books will tell you to stand with the canoe cradled on your thighs, get the right grip, and, with a decisive shove, flip it over your head. Don't! Women can do this alone, of course, but unless you have good upper-body strength and some athletic confidence, you won't have the conviction to pull off this maneuver. Instead, two or three people can do it together (knees bent!), dropping the canoe onto one person's shoulders for carrying.

Lift just one end. Lifting and twisting simultaneously is what can send you off to the chiropractor, so divide up these two motions, and lift

The art of portage.

just half the canoe. Here's the method used by friends from Iowa who have canoed hundreds of miles together—and since no one had ever told them the Correct Way, they invented this logical one. Turn the canoe upside down (with the ends on grass or shrubs so it won't get scratched up). Two women stand on opposite sides of the bow and lift that end only. One then supports the bow end while the other moves into carrying position. When you do this solo, lift the stern and then walk your way forward to the yoke.

Cartopping. I've seen several devices to aid in loading canoes, but I'm not convinced by them. The best apparatus (which you'll want anyway if you own a good canoe) is a high-quality cartop carrier. If you're loading your canoe single-handedly, walk it up behind the car, rest the bow on the back rack, and then slide the canoe forward. This works well on rubber-coated pipe racks (I sometimes cover the pipe with plumber's insulating foam, duct-taped on, which rotates as the canoe slides forward). Carriers that use 2x4s can be covered with carpet remnants to protect beautiful wood gunwales.

Solo Canoes

A few years ago solo canoeing meant taking a double canoe for a spin by yourself. (If you do this, sit near the middle. If you sit in the stern, the bow will be high out of the water, blown around by the wind.) These days, however, we have available real solo boats, elegantly designed for speed or maneuverability. They solve the problem of finding partners who have the same free time as you. You learn faster. And solo canoes are fun—the best way to experience the grace and freedom of canoeing. Compared to the flat-bottomed outfitter-fleet canoes most people know, they are like driving a Porsche, not a Chevy truck. If you don't have time for two-week or even weekend trips, these boats will entice you out for an evening paddle on a little stream or city lake. For all these reasons women really like solo canoes.

Styles of Canoeing and Gear

Some people want to cover distance fast; others want to load up a month's food and gear. A few want to play around in little streams. There is no one "all-around" canoe—if it goes fast and straight, for instance, it won't turn well. If you are buying, you have to try out a lot of models first to see what you like. Don't be put off by gear snobs: A good canoe is one you can own and use and *any* canoe on the water is worth two in the store. However, if all you have ever used is a large flat-bottomed aluminum canoe, at least try out solo boats or slender, faster tandem boats of more graceful lines.

Long before buying a canoe, get your own lightweight paddle, since most rental paddles are terrible aluminum-plastic clunkers. Get your own life jacket, too, and not the kind with flat panels—look for many soft segments and pockets. A comfortable one works better—you'll be wearing it more often.

A Quick Look at Some Other Water Sports

Sea kayaking. Lately, some of my canoe pals have been defecting to sea kayaks, and it's not just because kayaking is very "in" these days. As good canoe areas get more crowded (or remain very remote and expensive), sea kayaks are a good way to seek relatively accessible solitude. I asked my colleague Gail Green, who's been teaching sea kayaking for years, whether she thought kayaking is different for women and men. Oh, yes, she said. "Women and water are an age-old fit, aqueous rhythms in harmony. Women access our emotions differently than men—I think we can immediately see kayaking as a means to take us to the places that are going to connect us to the earth, and to ourselves, and not get stuck in overvaluing the skills."

When it comes to learning those skills, good instruction from the beginning is even more important than in canoeing. So is gear that is sized for women, since the idea is to "wear your boat." Women, Gail says, need to look for equipment built with women's body sizes in mind, and learn to customize the fit. "Seek effective, supportive learning environments to be introduced to the sport. You only have your first time once. Treasure it and be sure everything is optimal—you want to do this for the rest of your life."

Rafting. I'm saying nothing of technique here, because rafting isn't my sport and because, unlike canoeing or kayaking, rafting *skill* is predominantly the business of paid guides, where passengers follow directions and hang on. One thing worth considering: Many sports develop around them an entire culture and lifestyle; in this case a wild desert-rat, devil-may-care style is common among raft guides. My desert-rat friends tell me the old drink-and-dope scene is being considerably cleaned up these days; tours now range from teaching a lot about desert environments, to haute cuisine, to pure Yee-Haw! If you are booking a commercial raft trip, ask a lot of questions to find the style that appeals to you.

Sailing is beyond the range of this camping book, but it's worth mentioning that a recent sailing guide for women (see Resources, below) lists a dozen women's programs and events—and this doesn't include several others I know of as well as many more small local companies around the country. What's typical of the sailors I've worked with, and other women's brochures I've seen, is reference to avoiding the autocratic captain, the Captain Bligh Syndrome. If you're out to have fun learning to sail, who needs that? "Nobody yells," they say.

Resources

CANOE INSTRUCTION

Gullion, Laurie. *Canoeing: a Woman's Guide.* Camden, Maine: Ragged Mountain Press, 1998.

Mason, Bill. *The Path of the Paddle.* 1983. Reprint,: Minnetonka, Minn.: Cowles Creative Publishing, 1995.

The Path of the Paddle: Quietwater and *The Path of the Paddle: Whitewater.* VCR; each 60 minutes. Produced by Bill Mason. Toronto: Canadian Film Board, 1997. Available from North Sound Music, P.O. Box 1360, Minocqua, WI 54548. www.northsoundmusic.com.

WOMEN'S CANOE TRAVELS

Many more titles are listed in Jan Brown's bibliography; see the appendix.

Fons, Valerie. *Keep It Moving: Baja by Canoe.* Seattle: The Mountaineers, 1986. Classic story of a woman who drops her previous life to join adventurer Verlen Kruger on "the Ultimate Canoe Challenge."

Niemi, Judith, and Barbara Wieser, eds. *Rivers Running Free: Stories of Adventurous Women.* 1987. Reprint, Seattle: Seal Press, 1997. Thirty-six canoewomen, from 1900 to the present, write about freedom, companionship, learning, and wilderness.

Sutherland, Audrey. *Paddling My Own Canoe*. Honolulu: University of Hawaii Press, 1978. The author started off swimming the wild waters of the north coast of Moloka'i, finally got an inflatable canoe, and started a life of travels. Her motto:"Go light, go alone, go now!"

SEA KAYAKING

Jason, Victoria. *Kabloona in a Yellow Kayak*. Winnipeg:Turnstone Press, 1995. Four summers of travel through the entire Northwest Passage—the first two with an egomaniacal companion, the last two solo and far safer.

Johnson, Shelley. *Sea Kayaking:A Woman's Guide*. Camden, Maine: Ragged Mountain Press, 1998.

Linnea,Ann. *Deep Water Passage:A Spiritual Journey at Midlife*. Boston: Little, Brown, 1995. The author's nine-week trip around Lake Superior, sometimes with her friend Paul, sometimes solo.

RAFTING

Fans of Meryl Streep in *The River Wild* will be interested to know she actually ran many of the rapids, not leaving it all to stuntwomen, who say she was pretty good.You'll find more stories of women in the rafting world of the Southwest in:

Teal, Louise. *Breaking into the Current: Boatwomen of the Grand Canyon*. Tuscon: University of Arizona Press, 1994.Well-written interviews with eleven river guides.

The other aspect of rafting is the magnificent country you travel:

McCairen, Patricia C. *Canyon Solitude:A Woman's Solo Journey through the Grand Canyon*. Seattle: Seal Press, 1998.

Meloy, Ellen. *Raven's Exile: A Season on the Green River*. New York: Henry Holt, 1994.

SAILING

Colgate, Doris. *Sailing: A Woman's Guide*. Camden, Maine: Ragged Mountain Press, 1999.

Land Travels and Activities

This is just a quick survey to encourage you to think about what suits you. It may not work to just take up whatever activities your friends or families already do; outdoor life, if it becomes your passion, is a highly individual choice. Some people need to be around water to feel calm and whole. Maybe you're happiest high in the mountains, trying to leave earth behind. Or you enjoy most the company of other species (or hate being a beast of burden yourself) and will love dogsledding or hiking with llamas. This chapter will look at a few "silent sports" and forms of nonmotorized travel, with encouragement and advice from women who teach these skills and hints on how to find information for women.

Hiking and Backpacking

Walking your own way. Walking is so personal that our speech is full of phrases that recognize its importance and individuality: We demonstrate our convictions in marches, joining with others "from all walks of life," and we empathize with others by "walking a mile in their shoes." Becoming a good walker means finding your own natural pace. Height-weight-age charts won't tell you how fast you should walk. It depends not only on your physical size and condition, but also on your temperament. To find your own pace, walk. Do it a lot, preferably alone. On perhaps the third or fourth day of a hiking trip, or after a couple of weeks' worth of walks around your neighborhood, you'll "hit your stride," and you'll know it. You feel alive and energetic; you could go on all day. Pay attention to that feeling, cultivate it and recognize it, so you'll get used to walking at your own pace, not anyone else's.

Walking with others. Walking your own pace feels wonderful, but playing catch-up, when short-legged people and long-legged people hike together, can be miserable. Wonder why short-legged people get tired? Lynn Thomas (*The Backpacking Woman*, 1980) estimates that while a 6-foot man with a 3-foot stride covers a mile in 1,760 steps, a short woman might have to take 3,520 steps, or up to 5,000 if she's hurrying. It's not fun; it's also not very enjoyable for long-legged people to constantly try to shorten their stride or wait. Something's got to give.

Faster hikers can go their own way and periodically stop to wait, staying busy with maps, bird watching, whatever. (Fast walkers must *not* take off as soon as the slower ones come into sight. This causes all kinds of bad feelings. And all hikers carry their own snacks and water! Your feeling of freedom is ruined if your lunch has gone way ahead.) If each person is competent and confident enough, you can enjoy hiking separately all day, only meeting up at agreed-upon campsites. Or instead of always planning straight-line or circle routes, you can hike in to a base camp and from there take day hikes that accommodate different paces and wishes. If you hike with kids, you'll really have to adjust for short legs—and for children's habit of stopping to investigate everything. Maybe they know something about the reason for walking that many of us have forgotten.

Backyard backpacking. Before setting off for famous mountain trails, high altitudes, or rough terrain, ease into backpacking. Break in your boots. Test what weight you can carry, and find out how much you can live without. Get in shape by walking to work or on errands. A professor friend of mine used to get in shape for the Sierras by filling his pack with books and hiking up and down the stairs in his apartment building, while grading history exams. Many of us don't have that kind of discipline (and I never did ask if his grading got tougher or more lenient by the tenth floor). But you can make conditioning your excuse for great weekend getaways.

I asked backpacking leader Linda Getz what would be her most essential advice to beginning backpackers. Now, Linda loves far away places so much that she took a year off work to celebrate turning fifty by hiking in the Sierras, Nepal, and Alaska. But her immediate response was, "I'm always telling people, use backpacking to get into wild places close to home. Even in crowded state and national parks, while other people were being turned away, I've gotten in just by saying that I'm backpacking. Often there are good 'backcountry' sites less than a mile from the road. And no radios or noise."

Getting a Good Fit

Good boots or shoes are essential (see chapter 8), but "good" isn't what a salesclerk recommends, it's what fits your feet. (Unfortunately, that makes it hard to take advantage of great mail-order sales.) For many women this means buying from a company that builds boots on a woman's last. Packs, too, are not really gender-free. Don't get one too large. You will normally carry only twenty to twenty-five pounds of gear (weigh everything!), plus about a pound and a half of food per day. So it's not just total carrying capacity that matters—you want a frame that fits your bone structure. Several companies now build packs to women's dimensions. Whether you want an internal-frame pack (balances better) or an external-frame (cooler in hot weather) is up to you. In either, look for a well-padded hip belt, to take full advantage of women's wider hips; this allows the weight to be carried on your pelvic bones, not just on your shoulders and neck.

Rockclimbing and Mountaineering

Strength isn't everything. One image of rock climbing comes from magazine photos—a climber in hot pink and black tights hangs by one straining, sinewy arm over thousands of feet of empty space. And in recent years, it may well be a woman in that photo.

"Not for me!" you think. But only a small percentage of climbers are super-athletes, and most climbing is done with many safeguards. You can enjoy climbing and mountaineering at many levels with just general good health and moderate fitness.

"Actually, physical strength is hardly important at all, in any way, for beginning climbers," says Melissa Quigley, a competition climber and climbing instructor. "It's fun to watch women as they discover that upper-body strength doesn't matter, as they learn the tricks and techniques. It's grace, and finding your center of balance." In fact, Melissa believes women may have an advantage in learning climbing. "Some men when beginning just pull themselves up, like climbing a ladder without using their legs. They are so strong, they don't take time to learn the techniques, to learn the dance. Women often have a better sense of their bodies, and they have to learn the dance, the balance—it's actually more beautiful to watch."

In climbing and other outdoor activities that involve danger, it's important to get good instruction. This can come from friends or informal clubs, but you're likely to make better progress with a qualified teacher. Don't be reluctant to ask for and check references, to inquire about safety records. Should you look for a woman instructor or a women's class? Some instructors believe that they tend not to push their students as hard in an all-women's group. Melissa finds the opposite. "When it's an all-women's group, women tend to have lots of personal interaction and be much more supportive. So they try harder; there's more chance of working through the fear."

Mountaineering—a women's tradition. Women have been enthusiastic mountaineers since the earliest days of the sport, when they climbed in skirts and hobnailed boots, cutting out snow steps with a tin drinking cup. Mountaineering is also about the best-documented of all outdoor adventures. Are climbers more literary, or less private, than other outdoorspeople, or is it just that the drama of mountain stories makes good reading? Whatever the reason, there is a rich literature about women and mountains, and even if you'd never dream of taking up mountain climbing, these books make for inspirational reading on the spirit of adventure in women. (See Resources at the end of this chapter for some suggestions.)

Bicycling

A sense of history. Bicycling was all the rage about a century ago, but when women enthusiastically joined in, some people became really upset. Conservative gentlemen foresaw (quite correctly) that freedom of movement for women could lead . . . well, who knew where? So they raised all kinds of objections: Learned men proclaimed that bicycling was bad for a lady's heart, delicate female organs, and fragile mental health. They were trying to hold back the tide. Today women outnumber men as buyers of bicycles. When you get your bike out, don't just think about the good it's doing your heart and mental health—recapture the rebellious sense of freedom of those early riders in bloomers, or your own ten-year-old self with your first bike.

Girls' bikes. Since we no longer have to maintain standards of femininity by riding in long skirts, the "women's frame" (or drop frame) is a matter of tradition, not real function. The question is whether you're comfortable swinging your leg over the seat. An elderly gentleman was asked by some busybody why he rode a "women's bike." He said, with great dignity, "*This* is a man's step-through." Many models of bicycles are not made with drop frames. Bicycle frames are not, however, unisex in design. Most of them are proportioned to average men's bodies.

Women usually come with shorter torsos, shorter arms, and smaller hands; among the problems bike designs have caused many women is a tired neck, from leaning too far forward over a front tube that is too long for them. Mechanical engineer Georgene Terry, a builder of custom bicycle frames, found that most of her customers were women, who liked her design features. Besides a shorter top tube, her bikes have smaller handlebars, toe clips, and brake levers; on short bikes good balance also requires a front wheel smaller than the rear one. She began marketing a line of Terry bikes in 1985. Some other manufacturers now also incorporate designs that fit many women's bodies better. Mountain bicycles, which have brought bicycling off the highways and into the backcountry, are often available in drop-frame design, and some are now available in compact models.

Winter Sports

Staying warm. The ability to tolerate cold well is partly genetic. Women have an inherent advantage in having a better layer of body fat for insulation, although this alone won't keep you warm unless you also pay attention to the other factors. These are: getting acclimated (your body takes care of this in time); being in good condition so your body can quickly convert food into heat (training conditions not only muscles, but also your metabolism); and knowing a hundred little tricks of dressing and behavior that keep you warm.

The body fat, acclimating and conditioning are up to you. Here are a few of the tricks:

◆ **Clothing.** Following fashion usually will ensure that you are cold. Be prepared to look bulky or bizarre. Approximately spherical is the right shape for really cold weather. Silly hats and enormous boots can also be crucial. (See chapter 8 for more details.)

◆ **Eating and drinking.** Even if you ordinarily eat only salads and lean fish, come prepared for winter activity with lots of high-cal snacks: peanut butter, nuts, chocolate, seeds, dried fruit, plum pudding, mincemeat. Drink a lot, but not caffeinated coffee or tea, and certainly not alcohol until later, in front of a warm fireplace. (That warm glow is only on the surface; alcohol is highly danger-ous in the cold. I think Saint Bernards really carry chicken soup in those little kegs.)

◆ **Don't sweat.** Take off layers, and pace yourself.

◆ **Don't ignore a chill.** Put on layers, jump around, eat something right away. At the first sign of frostbite, stop and warm the part. Fortunately, most women are not very inclined to tough it out, ignoring their body's signals. Reacting to cold is not being wimpy—it's a survival skill.

◆ **Use insulation when you find it.** When you have to stand around, look for wind shelter. Stand on wood instead of ice. Sit on a foam pad, extra clothing, grasses, anything at hand.

◆ **Be smart about your car.** If you drive to your destination, instead of turning up the heat in the car, keep it cooler, wear warmer clothes, and you'll be more ready for outdoor temperatures. Even if you don't want to learn one other thing about auto mechanics, learn all the tricks for starting your car in cold weather, and know how to jump-start it. Carry with you a winter kit: snow shovel, sand or kitty litter, a "space blanket" or sleeping bag, candles, snack food. Feel competent and ready for routine "emergencies."

Skiing. When you buy cross-country skis (or downhill skis), be sure to get knowledgeable advice. See to it that the salesperson considers not only your height and weight, but also how you are likely to ski—do you (at this stage) think you'll be a relaxed, easygoing skier or an aggressive, energetic one? It can make a difference in how flexible a ski you want. Most good ski boots will work well for men, but most women should ask for a boot made on a woman's last. Some women skiers are suggesting that boots, at least downhill boots, should also take into account that our balance is different. (We are more knock kneed; men are more bow legged.) Our center of gravity is also lower. Both of these can influence fine points of technique.

Snowshoeing. If you can shuffle around the house in old bedroom slippers, you can snowshoe. Not *well*, maybe—that will take some practice—but well enough to enjoy moving over the top of the snow, following animal tracks, photographing, walking the swamps you'd never enter in summer. Done this way, it's a sport that appeals to many women who love the outdoors but don't consider themselves athletic. Don't buy snowshoes that are unnecessarily big, especially not too wide.

Sled dogs. Both recreational mushing and sled-dog racing are becoming more popular, and women mushers have gotten much media attention.

The Iditarod is the most famous sled-dog race, a 1,000-mile run from Anchorage to Nome; after women won for four years straight (Libby Riddles in 1985 and Susan Butcher in 1986–88), Alaskans produced some fine T-shirts: ALASKA—WHERE MEN ARE MEN AND WOMEN WIN THE IDITAROD. ALASKA—HOME OF BEAUTIFUL DOGS AND FAST WOMEN. The longest race in the lower forty-eight, Minnesota's 500-mile John Beargrease Marathon, has seen three different women win it, setting records; Jamie Nelson has won it four times.

The joys of mushing.

Why are the women doing so well? Most women racers don't speculate in public. But many mushers, men and women, say the biggest asset many women have is their good relationship with the dogs, their patience as teachers. This is probably part of a long tradition of women as animal trainers. Back in 1927 a woman prospector in northern Manitoba surprised a journalist: "She holds rather original theories in dog training. None of her huskies has ever known the sting of the lash, yet they are devoted to her." Susan Butcher is said to be unmatched at knowing how dogs think; after a training run she may invite a dog indoors—to talk it over. Dee Dee Jonrowe, a noted Iditarod contender, once told a reporter that for many mushers, dog training is run like marine boot camp, but hers is "more like Girl Scout camp." When all other factors—good breeding, good training—are equal, she says it's the affection that makes the difference. Cooing and chirping to her dogs, she doesn't sound a bit like Sergeant Preston.

It's not that everyone should or can adopt women's ways of running dogs, or doing other sports. But the remarkable women mushers are for any woman a reminder that success comes from pursuing a sport the way that is natural to you, and that a woman's sensitivity, tact, and light touch are real assets in demanding outdoor activities.

Recent years have also brought about a huge growth in purely recreational mushing, and in northern states—Minnesota, Maine, Alaska—you'll find programs where a novice can spend a few days running dogs. Generally these teams are not racers, but accommodating, genial dogs accustomed to being driven by novices, tolerant of us.

Hunting and Fishing

Perhaps of all the outdoor skills, fishing and (especially) hunting are in our culture those that have been passed on to sons far more than daughters. Yet these are certainly ways that can foster an acute and detailed knowledge of the natural world.

Some ardent outdoorswomen, and many urban women, are adamantly opposed to hunting (some aren't much in sympathy with fishing, either). I'm not much of a partisan here, being only a casual fisher and not a hunter, but it seems worth pointing out that there are sportsmen and -women of the rod and gun who do far more than most of us to protect the habitat of the fish and game, and who pursue their activities with great respect. Slob hunters, those guys who drape a deer over their fender to show off, wasting the meat, we'll probably always have with us; we also have slob drivers, canoeists, skiers, mountaineers (littering Everest, Chomolungma). Especially if you eat meat, in any form, it's worth thinking about.

In 1991 Christine Thomas of the University of Wisconsin, Stevens Point, started a program called "Becoming an Outdoors-Woman," believing that women would prefer to learn about field sports from other women, in women's classes. BOW now offers weekend workshops in forty-seven states and many Canadian provinces, often in collaboration with state Departments of Natural Resources. The focus is on fishing and hunting skills, with a few workshops on other outdoor skills.

Animal Tracking—And Just Getting to Know the Nonhuman Neighbors

Some forms of nature observation have been long women's traditions—bird observation, for example, and birding is perhaps one of the few of these activities that can be practiced as a competitive sport, if you like life lists. Most people do their bird-watching, or fish-watching, or wildflower or fossil collecting in quiet, solitary ways. Tracking animals particularly is a skill that can be helped by books but is mostly acquired by patience, time, and observation. It can be a strenuous, active pursuit or a relatively sedentary one. It's most fun to practice it on sand beaches of big rivers where wolves, musk oxen, or grizzlies might have left stories, but there's interesting tracking in any snow-covered backyard, or along muddy urban riverbanks. Women become very interested when they realize that, with close observation and intuition, they can go for a walk with an animal, hours or days later, and learn something of its life.

I mention this because sometimes in our pursuit of outdoor skills we run the risk of getting too focused on our own technique, gear, and progress and forget the other reasons that we spend time outdoors. Perhaps the best reason is to gain perspective, to see ourselves as part of something larger. The best moments of sea kayaking or canoeing can be floating motionless on a glassy bay, watching fish shadows, or pulling ashore and smelling the presence of bears. My best skiing has been along trails pocked with the tracks of moose and wolves; my favorite camping places have been where beaver could be heard munching behind the tent, and in the morning their fresh trails showed where they had swished branches down to their own homes. Best of all is when the animals grow curious about us, tiptoe down the beach at dawn to check us out, and we're alert enough to say welcome.

Resources

BACKPACKING

Hall, Adrienne. *A Woman's Guide to Backpacking.* Camden, Maine: Ragged Mountain Press, 1998. Advice on gear, clothing, and how to get started.

ROCKCLIMBING AND MOUNTAINEERING

Gabbard, Andrea. *Mountaineering: A Woman's Guide.* Camden, Maine: Ragged Mountain Press, 1999.

Mountaineering literature is of great interest to many of us who wouldn't dream of going to high altitudes ourselves. Here are a few suggestions; Jan Brown's *Women Outdoors Bibliography* (see the appendix) can point you to many more.

Blum, Arlene. *Annapurna.* San Francisco: Sierra Club Books, 1999. A fine story of women's styles in mountaineering, with excerpts from journals of several women and an excellent annotated bibliography.

Da Silva, Rachel, ed. *Leading Out: Women Climbers Reaching for the Top*. Seattle: Seal Press, 1992.

Jackson, Monica, and Elizabeth Stark. *Tents in the Clouds: The First Women's Himalayan Expedition*. London, 1956. An impressive adventure of three Scottish women and a few Sherpas. Delightfully told with British humor and understatement.

Robertson, Janet. *The Magnificent Mountain Women: Adventures in the Colorado Rockies*. Lincoln: University of Nebraska Press, 1990.

BICYCLING

Murphy, Dervla. *Full Tilt: Ireland to India with a Bicycle*. 1965. Reprint, New York: Overlook Press, 1987.

———. *The Ukimwi Road: From Kenya to Zimbabwe*. 1993. Reprint, New York: Overlook Press, 1995. Mountain biking at age sixty through a continent ravaged by AIDS.

Ritchie, Andrew. *King of the Road: An Illustrated History of Cycling*. Berkeley: Ten Speed Press, 1975. Includes a fine chapter on "Women's Liberation" in English bicycling.

Savage, Barbara. *Off the Beaten Track*. Seattle: The Mountaineers, 1988.

SKIING AND SNOWBOARDING

High-tech sports are beyond the scope of this book, but it's worth mentioning that special workshops for women are an important part of this scene.

Carbone, Claudia. *Women Ski*. 2d ed. Boston: World Leisure Corporation, 1996. Covers anatomy and gear, and lists more than a hundred resorts with women's programs.

Carlson, Julia. *Snowboarding: A Woman's Guide*. Camden, Maine: Ragged Mountain Press, 1999. These days snowboarders claim to be the new wave (and next, I hear, it's ski-boarding). This book lists half a dozen all-women's snowboard instructional programs.

DOG MUSHING

Cook, Ann Mariah. *Running North: A Yukon Adventure*. Chapel Hill, N.C.: Algonquin Books, 1998. A New Hampshire couple moves to Alaska to prepare for his running the Iditarod. Good on their relationships with the sled dogs.

Riddles, Libby, with Tim Jones. *Race Across Alaska*. Mechanicsburg, Penn.: Stackpole Books, 1988. The inside story of the 1985 race, when the first woman won the Iditarod.

Shields, Mary. *Sled Dog Trails*. Anchorage: Pyrola Publishing, 1984. The first woman to finish the Iditarod writes about the race, and her everyday life with the dogs.

FISHING AND HUNTING

Rikimaru, Dana. *Fly Fishing: A Woman's Guide*. Camden, Maine: Ragged Mountain Press, 1999.

Thomas, Christine. *Becoming an Outdoors-Woman*. Helena, Mont.: Falcon Press, 1997. Personal adventures and misadventures along the author's way to learning. For information on how to contact the BOW programs in your area, see the appendix.

Fishing has been the source of a large body of writing respected as literature as well as far as its depth of information on this aspect of the natural world. A few of the more literary books, of interest whether or not you plan to take up the sport:

Grover, Jan Zita. *Northern Waters*. St. Paul: Graywolf Press, 1999. Essays on fishing, fish-watching, and learning about a place by learning its waters.

Legler, Gretchen. *All the Powerful, Invisible Things: A Sportswoman's Notebook*. Seattle: Seal Press, 1995. Personal essays on hunting and fishing, relationships, and life's changes.

Lord, Nancy. *Fish Camp*. Washington, D.C.: Island Press (Shearwater), 1997. This is about small-scale commercial salmon fishing, not sport fishing, but a lovely book about a life close to nature, and the cultural and economic issues surrounding a disappearing way of life.

Morris, Holly, ed. *A Different Angle: Fly Fishing Stories by Women*. Seattle: Seal Press, 1995.

———. *Uncommon Waters: Women Write about Fishing*. Seattle: Seal Press, 1991.

Schreiber, Le Anne. *Light Years: A Memoir*. New York: The Lyons Press, 1996. Essays on learning fly fishing and country life, on family and mortality.

Stange, Mary Zeiss. *Woman the Hunter*. Boston: Beacon, 1997. Academic study of the cultural history of hunting and personal narratives by a woman hunter.

TRACKING

Benyus, Janine. *The Field Guide to Wildlife Habitats of the Eastern United States*. New York: Simon and Schuster, 1989.

———. *Northwoods Wildlife*. Minocqua, Wis.: NorthWord, 1989.

Brown, Tom, with Brandt Morgan. *Field Guide to Nature Observation and Tracking*. New York: Berkley, 1983. Look for many other titles on the same subject, too.

Nyala, Hannah. *Point Last Seen: A Woman Tracker's Story*. Boston: Beacon, 1997. Combines stories of tracking lost people for the National Park Service with vignettes of the author's life as a battered woman and struggles to find her abducted children.

Rezendes, Paul. *Tracking and the Art of Seeing*. 2d ed. New York: HarperCollins, 1999.

———. *The Wild Within*. New York: Tarcher/Putnam, 1998.

Postscript: Don't Shop Till You Drop

The chill of winter has left and it's glorious high spring, a sunny Sunday afternoon filled with songs of migrating birds. And what are outdoor-minded people doing? Well, there's an immense herd of 4WD SUVs, with expensive bike and kayak racks on top, filling up the parking lot of our local REI store, a soaring temple of commerce. This is nuts! Resist the impulse to start any new phase of your outdoor life by buying gear. Get *outside!* Have fun, make mistakes, develop the skills and common sense that are more important than any piece of equipment. Along the way you'll find out what gear you really do want.

How New Outdoor Gear Comes into the World

Still, let's not be too cynical about the outdoor biz. There are infinitely more outdoor products than anyone needs, of course, but a lot of it is really good stuff. Here's what often happens. Some outdoor enthusiast applies know-how and new materials to solve his or her own specific problems and designs new climbing hardware, or mittens you can wear over your kayak paddle, or a really clever new tarp design. Often it starts with one inventive genius with an old sewing machine in the garage. The inventor becomes an entrepreneur, forms a small company called Whiffenpoof or Orca, and a clever new product is available to other hardcore campers who know why they "need" it. Then the small company grows and the inventor gets tired of managing—after all, she or he never planned to spend life in an office—and sells to a huge corporation. Now economies of scale require that the big corporation has to sell a lot of stuff, and has to convince a lot of people to want it, whether they need it or not.

Just Say No

If you're trying to resist a purchase, ask yourself:

◆ How did the human race get along without this until now? Think about less developed countries where local people use fewer things in a year than many Americans bring for two weeks of travel there. A few modern products are almost indispensable— say, plastic bags and duct tape. The rest is frills.

◆ Do I want it *now*? If sophisticated, top-of-the-line gear will help your learning, and you can afford it, fine. Don't get it if it's more than you can use. Will you feel upstaged by your own equipment, unnerved by too many gears on the bike, worried about keeping the expensive tent clean?

◆ Is a simple design better? Could I repair this in the field?

◆ Can I improvise? Invent and scrounge. Collect useful items: Nurses can supply used sterile saline bottles (water bottles, for storing milk powder or syrup); small plastic bottles are good for matches, spices, or soup powder.

Advice from the Field

I asked a lot of my camping friends, "What's your absolutely favorite piece of outdoor gear? The thing you can't imagine going camping without?" The answers tended to fall into two categories: sentimental attachments to gear that had traveled with them a long time—a Girl Scout knife from her father, an ancient hat she couldn't bear to throw out. Or mundane little improvisations: the insulated coffee mug with its lid fastened on with cord. Things that had acquired personal value.

While revising this book I took a day off to canoe the backwaters of the St. Croix River with six serious paddlers and a golden retriever. With us also were one beautiful new Kevlar canoe on its maiden voyage and one new, obscenely expensive, paddle. We hardly mentioned them. ("Like your new canoe?" "Oh, yeah.") What we talked about was turkey vultures and eagles and rue anemones and the governor's appointments and a lawsuit and pileated woodpeckers. Even if we'd had to rent the inelegant gear the local outfitter had, we'd have had almost as good a time.

The Gear Head

There are a couple of erroneous assumptions about "gear heads": First, they are all male and, second, they all have more toys than they have time to use 'em. The mark of the true gear head, the connoisseur, is not necessarily *owning,* however. The real point is to be able to *talk* about equipment, endlessly. If you do love outdoor gear, it's fairly inexpensive to play this part of the game. Outdoor magazines are always running reviews of new equipment. (After all, who pays their bills?) Pick up copies of *Canoe, Paddler, Backpacker,* or *Outside.* Then when you do buy gear, you'll know just what you want—or at least what questions to ask. (If technical details bore you, skip the reviews, but do get advice from experienced people.)

Where to Shop

For the best outdoor clothes, go to an outdoor store with a full range of serious outdoor clothing and equipment, not to a department store. The extra features make a difference: covered zippers, large pockets, sturdier construction. For tents and packs, too, shop the outdoor store, not discount stores or gas stations. Cheap gear is often no bargain. It won't last—because of narrow seam allowances, flimsy construction, bad zippers. Sometimes it never works well, because of bad design. Look for a store that deals in information as well as merchandise. If there are well-informed sales staff who are themselves enthusiastic outdoorspeople, go when it's not busy and ask a lot of questions.

For some of your gear, you can get by spending less. Army surplus gear varies wildly in quality, but you often get good value in basic packs, clothing, and cook kits. Cheap men's work clothes have worked for thousands of outdoorswomen. Small-town general stores and variety stores often have wool shirts, jackets, and leather gloves at much lower prices than urban camping stores. Name-brand gear is available at discounted or reasonable prices from several mail-order sources. Shop sales. Buy off season: skis in March, canoes in September and October. And check for used sporting goods stores, or trade-in departments; there's a lot of fine gear, cheap, from gear heads trading up.

Some Mail-Order Sources of Equipment

Campmor (800) 226-7667; www.campmor.com. Wide variety of clothing, gear, gadgets.

Patagonia (800) 638-6464. High-tech clothing, an informative catalog. Their toll-free Guide Line can answer your questions on gear, stores, destinations: (800) 523-9597.

REI (Recreational Equipment, Inc.) (800) 426-4840.

Sierra Trading Post (800) 713-4534.

Also, specialized winter gear that's not always easy to find is available from two small companies in Ely, Minnesota:

Steger Designs (800) 685-5857. Warm mukluks, custom-made anoraks, Lapp hats, expedition mitts.

Wintergreen (800) 584-9425. Expedition-quality parkas, hats, wind pants.

Getting Started in Gear

Prices quoted are about what you'll probably have to spend for low-end but quite decent gear, based on my rambling through mail-order catalogs at press time. Prices of course will vary depending on where you live, where you want to go, and when you begin this quest.

Step 1: Just Being Comfortable Outdoors

Besides your comfortable clothes, you should be sure to get:

◆ A good rainsuit (coated nylon is fine, not too tight; pants and jacket, not just a poncho): $40–100.

◆ Good walking shoes or light boots: $50–100. (But my last pair was $24—down from $70—at a good sale.)

◆ Quick-drying long pants with good pockets: $10–20 (army surplus) on up to $60.

◆ Pocketknife or pocket tool: $10 (cheap knockoff) to $40.

Step 2: Camping Out

◆ Sleeping bag, three season (don't buy one of those flannel-lined ones with ducks—but if you happen to have one, use it until a good buy comes along): $70–150.

◆ Tent, freestanding, with separate rainfly: $100–200.

◆ Camp stove, white gas: $40–70.

Step 3: The Gear of Your Chosen Activities

The sky's the limit, unfortunately. Consult the catalogs, magazines, and talk to people. Whenever possible, try before you buy. Rent what you can, and buy slowly, beginning with things important to your comfort and safety, or that have meaning to you.

Appendix

Some General Resources

Suggested readings on specific outdoor activities are included in each chapter. These are general sources for locating more books and other information.

Adventurous Traveler Bookstore, 245 South Champlain, Burlington, VT 05401; (800) 282-3963; fax (800) 677-1821; www.adventuroustraveler.com. Guidebooks and maps.

Becoming an Outdoors-Woman, Dr. Christine Thomas, College of Natural Resources, University of Wisconsin, Stevens Point, Stevens Point, WI 54481; (877) BO-WOMAN; www.state.nj.us/dep/fgw/bowhome.htm. Offers weekend workshops in most states and Canadian provinces, often in conjunction with Departments of Natural Resources. Fishing, hunting, and related outdoor skills.

GORP (Great Outdoor Reading and Provisions Co.), P.O. Box 3016, Everett, WA 98203-1016; (888) 994-4677; overseas (425) 355-8585; fax (425) 355-7131; www.trailstuff.com. Mail-order service for a wide variety of instruction books, trail guides, narratives.

Melpomene Institute, 1010 University Avenue, St. Paul, MN 55104; (651) 642-1951; fax (651) 642-1871; www.melpomene.org. Research and reports on women's wellness and athletics.

Totally Outdoors, www.totallyoutdoors.com. Mail-order gear especially for women, and links to some women's programs.

Women in the Wilderness, Judith Niemi, 566 Ottawa Avenue, St. Paul, MN 55107; (651) 227-2284; fax (651) 227-4028. Besides offering trips, sells selected books and videos on outdoors skills for women and women adventurers.

Women Outdoors, 55 Talbot Avenue, Medford, MA 02155. National network with local chapters. Dues $15 per year. Small quarterly journal, annual get-together, and offers some valuable reports:

◆ Jan Brown's splendid and extensive *Women Outdoors Bibliography* is cross-referenced by region, sport, and topics. Annotated. 90 pages, 1998 edition. You can find literature on whatever your own outdoor interests are (family adventure, country living, older women, women with disabilities . . .). $6.00 includes postage.

◆ *Women's Outdoor Programs.* This list is not always up to date or accurate, but it's the most ambitious effort I've seen to track outdoor programs (over three hundred are listed). $2.00.

Women's Outdoor Network, P.O. Box 50003, Palo Alto, CA 94303; (650) 494-8583; fax (650) 712-9093; www.earthlink.net/-wonforfun; e-mail wonforfun@earthlink.net.

Women's Sports Foundation, Eisenhower Park, East Meadow, NY 11554; (800) 227-3988; fax (516) 542-4716; www.lifetimetv.com/WoSport. Information and referral service.

Index

About the Author

Judith Niemi has been teaching women wilderness skills since the 1970s, when no one had heard of women's outdoor programs. She first founded Woodswomen and then Women in the Wilderness, based in St. Paul; she has led trips, usually involving canoeing, in the Arctic and the Amazon rain forest as well in her home country, northern Minnesota. She is coeditor of *Rivers Running Free*, an anthology of women's canoe stories, and has written many essays, articles, and a video.